# HAWORTH

## HISTORY TOUR

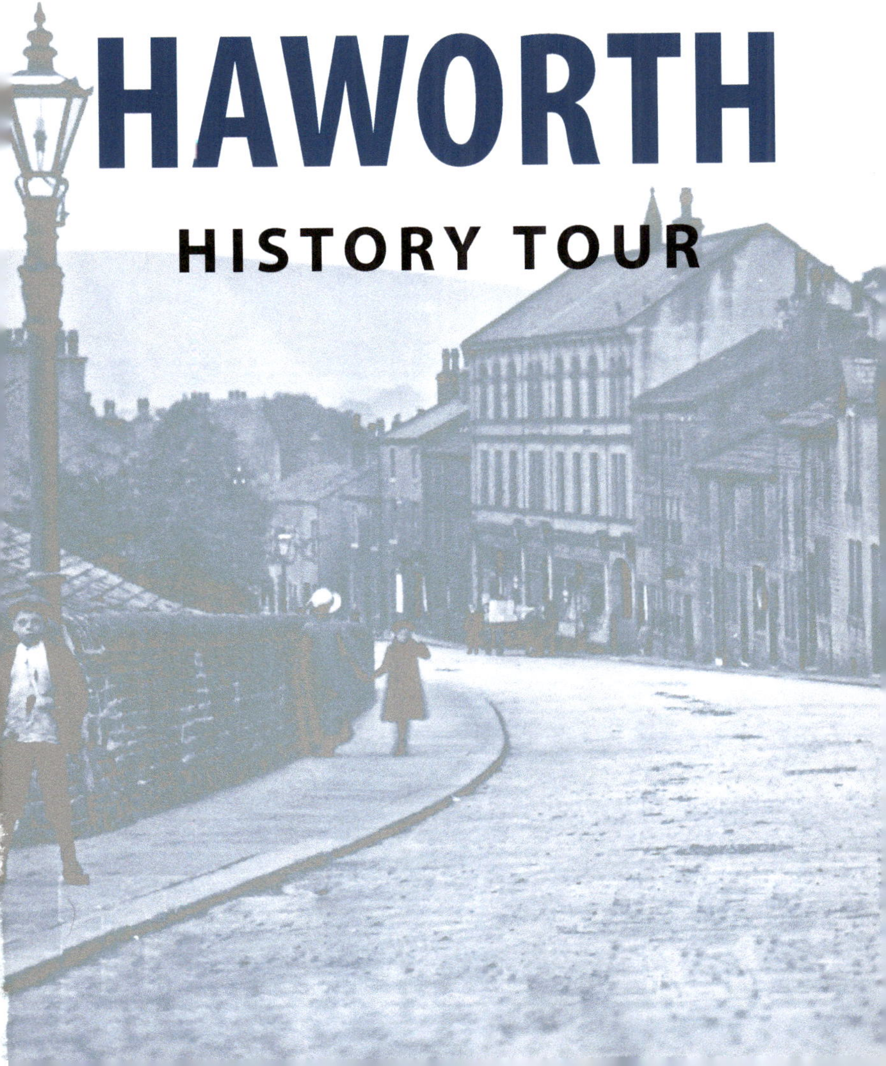

First published 2015

Amberley Publishing
The Hill, Stroud,
Gloucestershire, GL5 4EP
www.amberley-books.com



ISBN  978 1 4456 4627 5 (print)
ISBN  978 1 4456 4628 2 (ebook)



British Library Cataloguing in
Publication Data.
A catalogue record for this book is
available from the British Library.

Typesetting by Amberley Publishing.
Printed in Great Britain.

Appointed GPSR EU Representative:
Easy Access System Europe Oü,
16879218
Address: Mustamäe tee 50, 10621,
Tallinn, Estonia
Contact Details: gpsr.requests@
easproject.com, +358 40 500 3575

# INTRODUCTION

Haworth is famed mostly for the Brontë family. They were here for 40 years but the village has probably been here for a thousand years. It is a Pennine village that made its living from farming, stone quarrying and textile manufacture. Because of the interest in the Brontës it has been more photographed than most small towns, but the photographs have mostly been of the church and parsonage. I have tried to bring together a selection of old photographs (from the 1860s to the 1970s) that give a more representative picture of the place.

Change over the centuries has been brought by a number of factors. The making of the Blue Bell Turnpike through Haworth in 1755 probably caused the initial development of Main Street and linked the settlements of Hall Green at the bottom and Haworth at the top. There are a great many Nonconformist chapels in the Haworth area, partly because William Grimshaw, one of the leaders of the evangelical revival of the eighteenth century, was minister here.

A second turnpike road was built in 1814 from Lees to Hebden Bridge; this later formed the upper limit of development on Haworth Brow. The first gas works was built in 1857. The opening of a branch railway from Keighley in 1867 must have given an impetus to trade and started a major expansion of the village in the later nineteenth century. It also necessitated a number of changes in the roads serving the lower part of the village. In the 1870s, several large reservoirs were constructed in the upper Worth Valley to supply Keighley and Bradford with water. The effect of these was mostly felt by the farmers, although it had implications for the mills as well. The collapse of the Yorkshire Dales lead mining industry and a widespread agricultural depression elsewhere brought many families into the area in the 1880s and 1890s.

The first half of the twentieth century saw some new housing built, streets widened and roads surfaced with tarmac. Electricity began to replace gas, at least for lighting, in the 1930s.

The pace of change accelerated in the second half of the twentieth century. Two large areas of older housing were demolished in the name of slum clearance. A new road bypassed Main Street and the Mytholmes route from Haworth to Oakworth was greatly improved.

Indeed the growth in ownership of cars has been one of the most potent causes of change. The railway closed but was soon reopened by a preservation society. The quarries worked more sporadically and eventually all but one closed. The textile mills closed one by one; today only a single mill still produces specialist narrow fabrics. The smaller farms went out of business until now all the agriculture is concentrated in a small number of larger farms.

As the industry died out, Haworth became a more desirable place to live. More and more people travelled out of the village to work in Keighley and Bradford. There have been large new housing developments over the past few decades to meet the needs of incomers and smaller families. With the advent of supermarkets in neighbouring large towns people now do most of their shopping elsewhere and local shops have closed. Many of those that survive now cater for tourists rather than residents.

I hope that these photographs will illustrate at least some of the trends which have changed Haworth over the years.

I should add a note about the new photographs. Ian Palmer has taken great pains to reproduce the views in the old pictures but this has not always been possible. New buildings and the growth of trees were significant problems. Traffic was a constant difficulty got over only with much patience – and some daring! New street furniture has made many of Ian's photographs less pleasing than they might have been, but the old photographs, rather than aesthetic considerations, dictated what had to be taken.

Steven Wood
Haworth

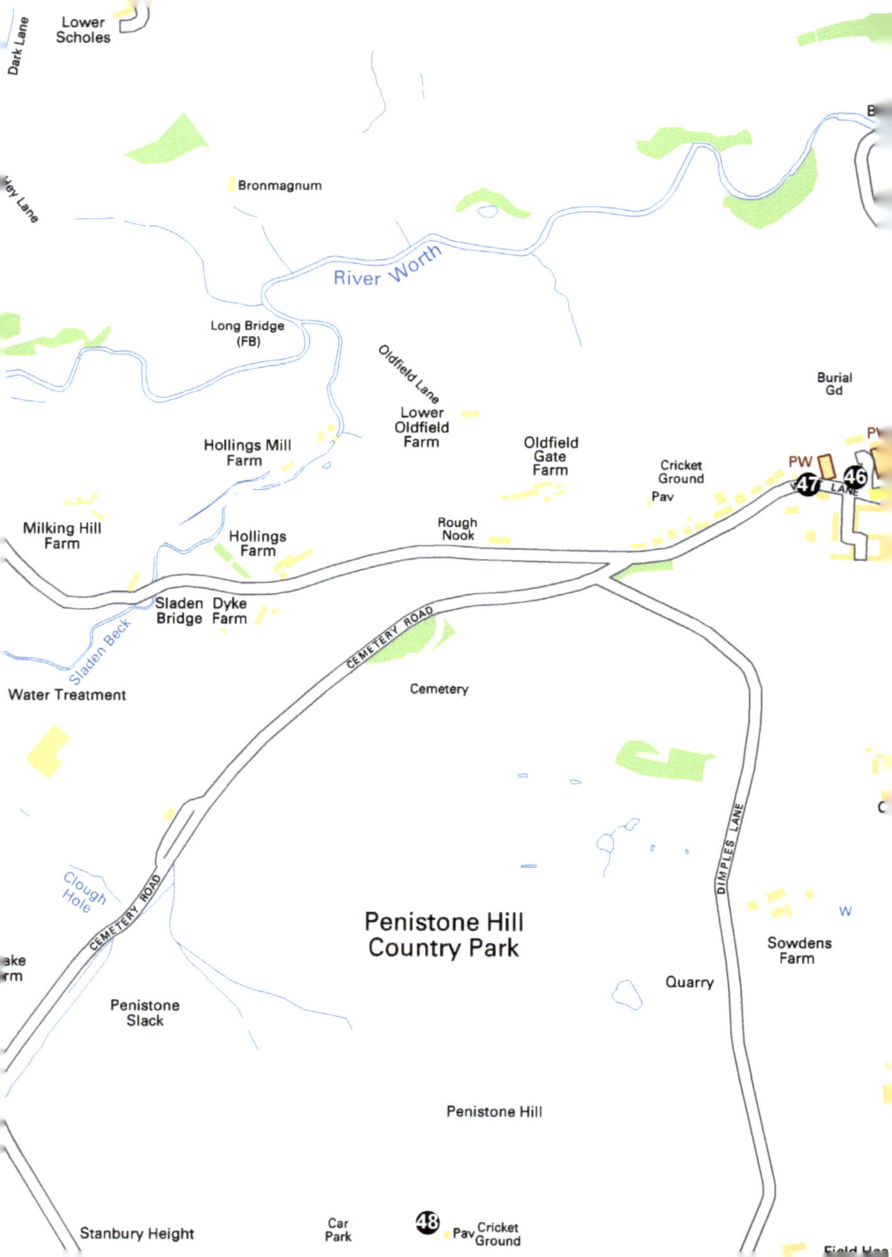

Dark Lane
Lower Scholes
Bronmagnum
ey Lane
River Worth
B
Long Bridge (FB)
Oldfield Lane
Lower Oldfield Farm
Burial Gd
Hollings Mill Farm
Oldfield Gate Farm
Cricket Ground
Pav
PW
PW
47
46
LANE
Milking Hill Farm
Hollings Farm
Rough Nook
Sladen Bridge
Dyke Farm
Sladen Beck
CEMETERY ROAD
Water Treatment
Cemetery
DIMPLES LANE
W
Clough Hole
Penistone Hill Country Park
Sowdens Farm
ake rm
CEMETERY ROAD
Quarry
Penistone Slack
C
Penistone Hill
Stanbury Height
Car Park
48
Pav
Cricket Ground
Field He

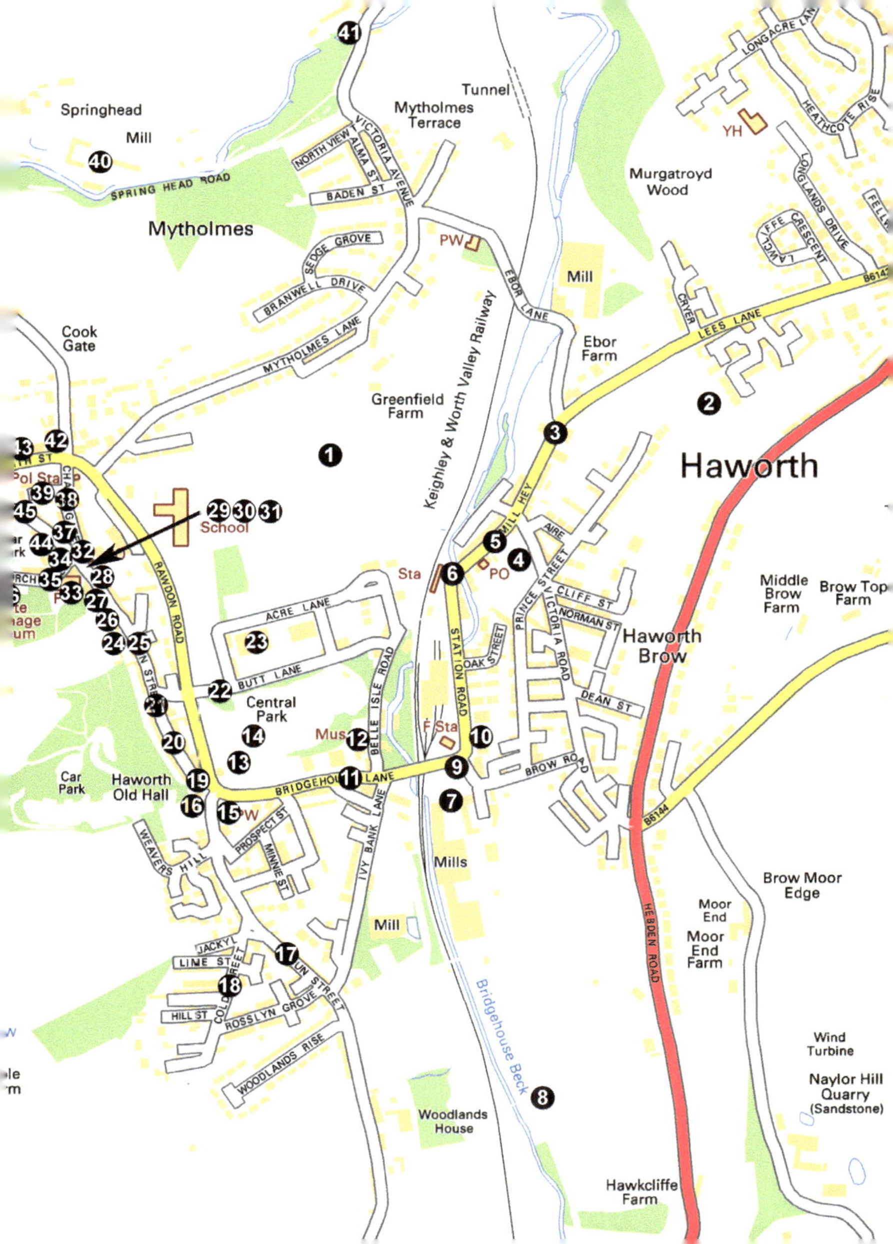

Springhead
Mill
Mytholmes
Cook
Gate
40
SPRING HEAD ROAD
NORTH VIEW
ALMA ST
VICTORIA AVENUE
BADEN ST
SEDGE GROVE
BRANWELL DRIVE
MYTHOLMES LANE
Tunnel
Mytholmes
Terrace
PW
Keighley & Worth Valley Railway
EBOR LANE
Mill
Ebor
Farm
Murgatroyd
Wood
YH
LONGACRE LANE
HEATHCOTE RISE
LYCETT CRESCENT
LONGLANDS DRIVE
FELL
CRYER
LEES LANE
B6142
Greenfield
Farm
2
3
Haworth
41
43
42
Pol Sta
CHAP
39
38
45
37
44
32
34
28
35
33
27
26
24 25
23
ACRE LANE
BUTT LANE
22
21
Central
Park
14
13
20
19
16
15 PW
Haworth
Old Hall
Car
Park
WEAVERS HILL
PROSPECT ST
MINNIE ST
29 30 31
School
RAWDON ROAD
N STREET
Sta
6
5
4
PO
MILL HEY
AIRE
PRINCE STREET
VICTORIA ROAD
CLIFF ST
NORMAN ST
Haworth
Brow
OAK STREET
STATION ROAD
Mus
12
BELLE ISLE ROAD
F Sta
10
9
11
BRIDGEHOUSE LANE
IVY BANK LANE
7
DEAN ST
BROW ROAD
Middle
Brow
Farm
Brow Top
Farm
B6144
HEBDEN ROAD
Brow Moor
Edge
Moor
End
Moor
End
Farm
Mills
Mill
17
18
JACKY
LIME STREET
COLD STREET
HILL ST
SUN STREET
ROSSLYN GROVE
WOODLANDS RISE
Bridgehouse Beck
Woodlands
House
8
Wind
Turbine
Naylor Hill
Quarry
(Sandstone)
Hawkcliffe
Farm

# 1. HAWORTH FROM BROW

Ivy Bank mill with its smoking chimney is visible on the left – it is now a burnt out ruin and the chimney has gone. The six houses on Ivy Bank Lane are prominent and date this picture to before 1890 when another six were built.

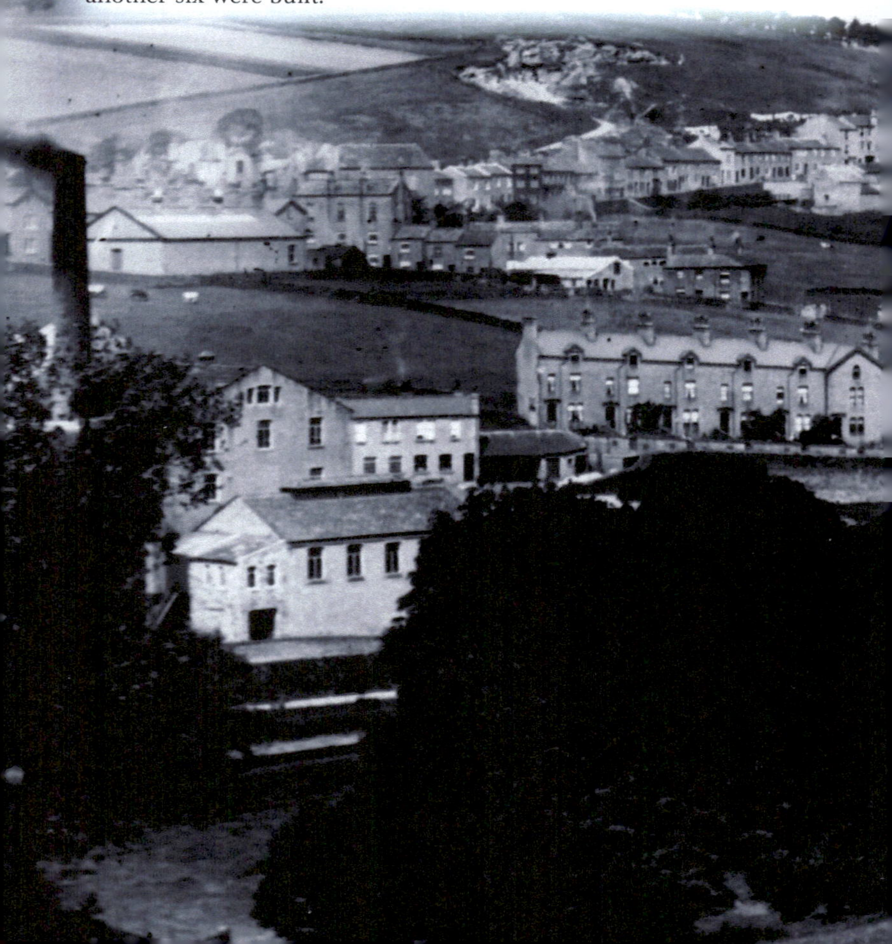

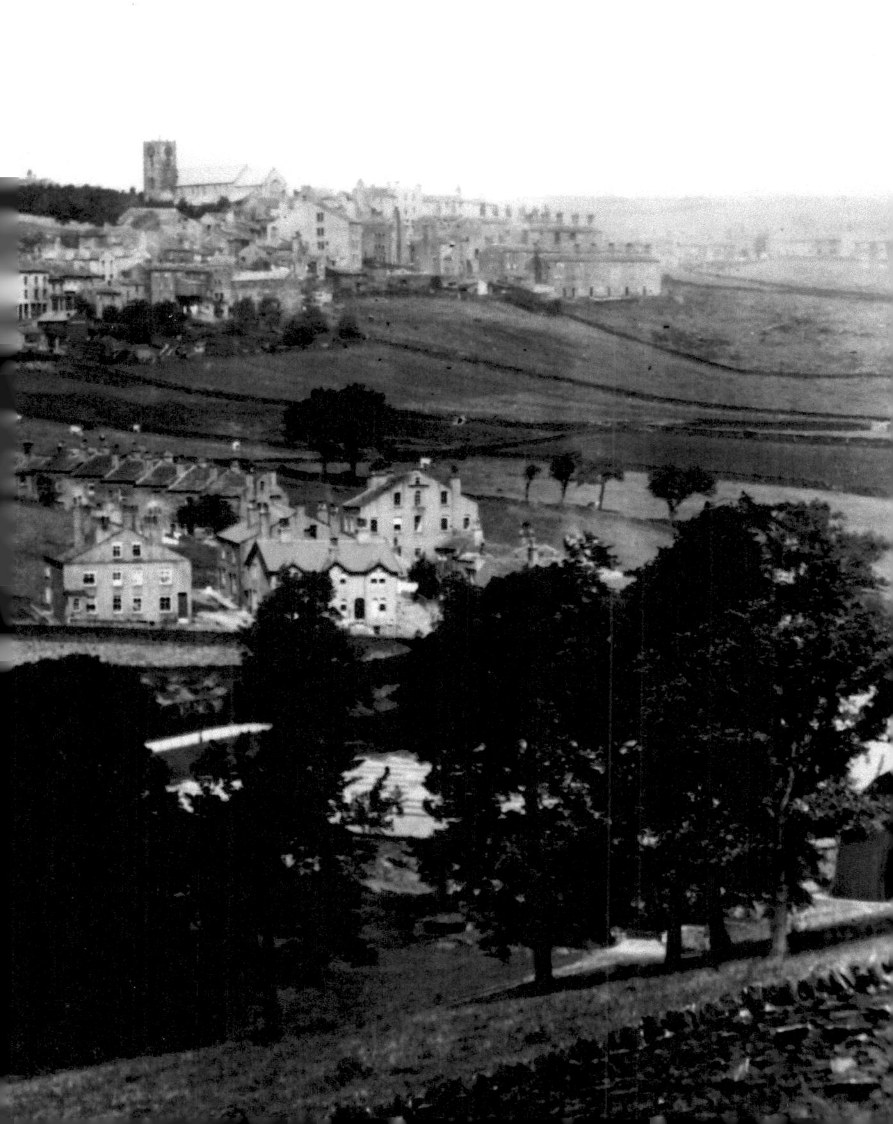

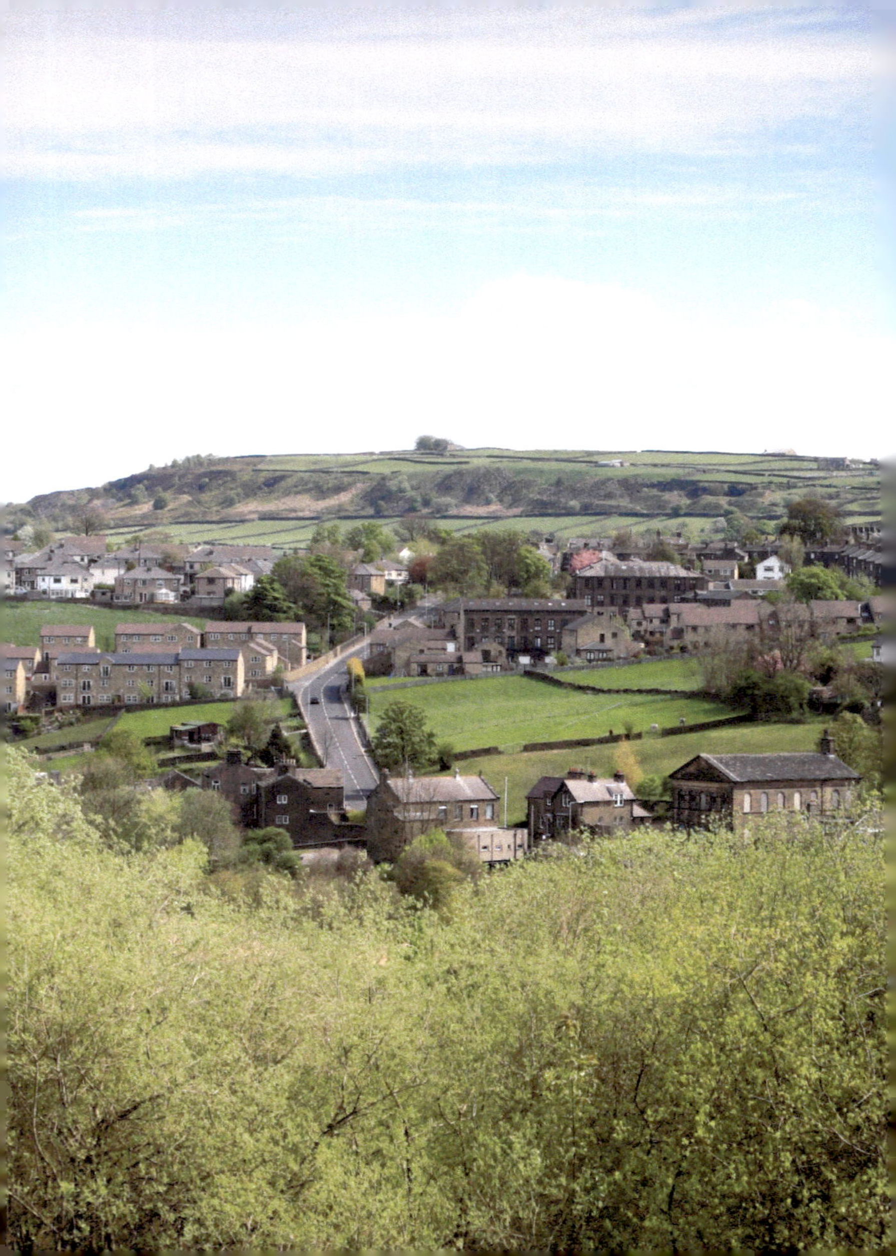

# 2. HAWORTH BROW

The extent of late nineteenth-century building is well seen in these general views of Haworth Brow. The Brow developed in the 1880s and 1890s and attracted immigrant workers from Swaledale, where the lead mines were closing, and from Wiltshire, which was suffering from the agricultural recession. The chimney on the right belongs to the 1857 Haworth gas works.

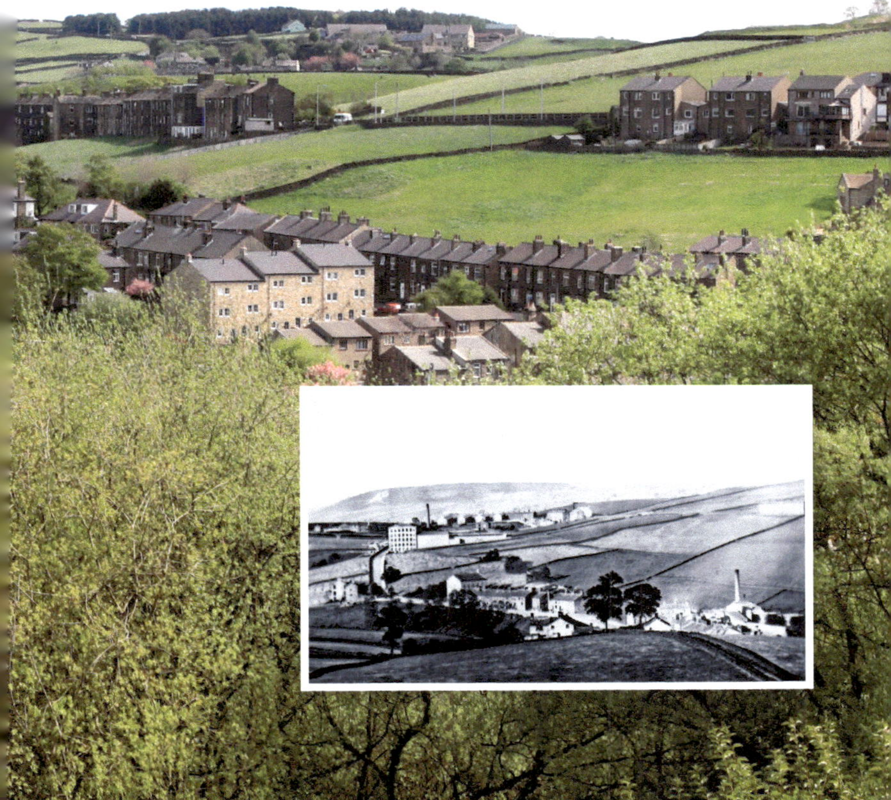

# 3. POLICE STATION, MILL HEY

Haworth's police station and masonic lodge face each other across Mill Hey. They were both built in 1907. A police officer can be seen standing outside the station while three boys stand in the road watching the photographer at work. Ebor House, which is largely obscured by a tree, was the mill owner's house for Ebor Mill. Just visible in the distance is Longlands, Haworth's Youth Hostel.

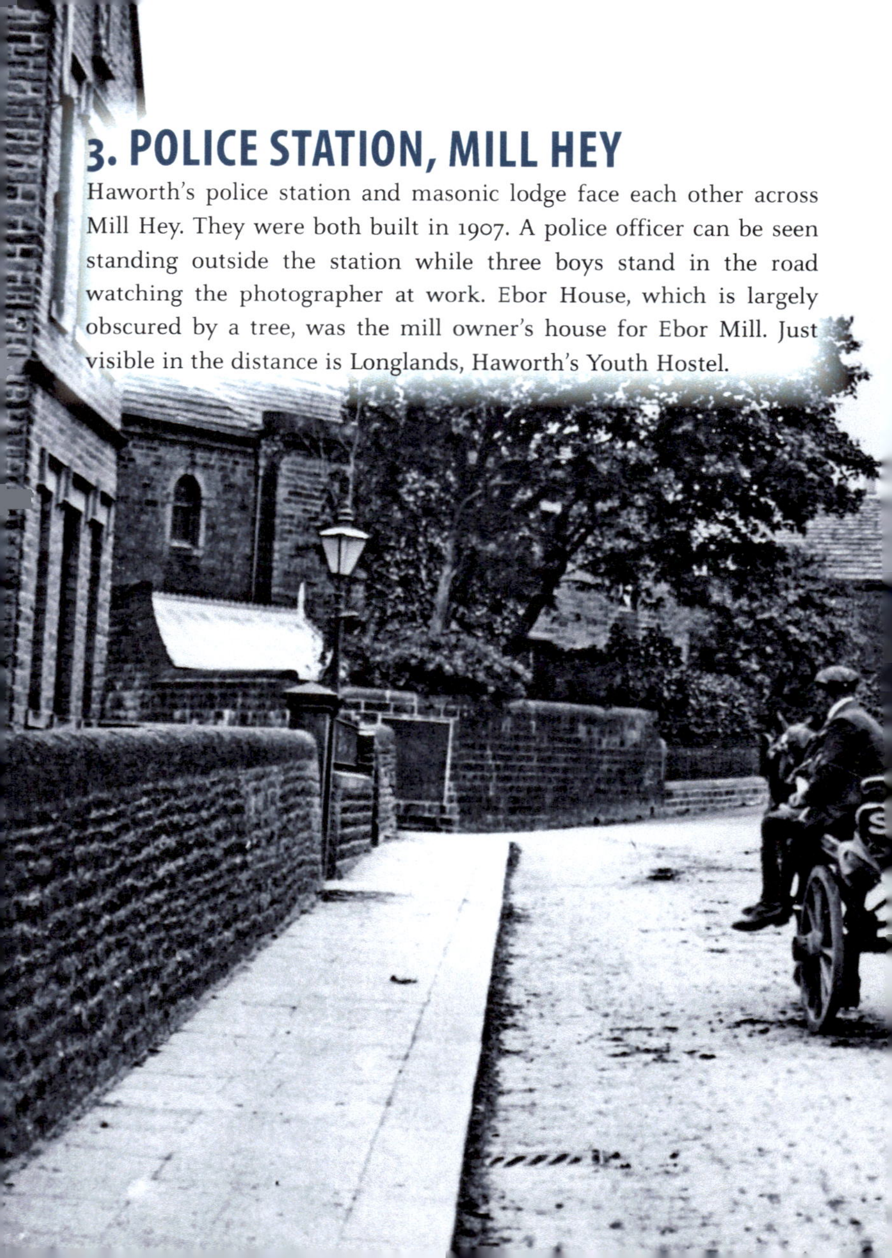

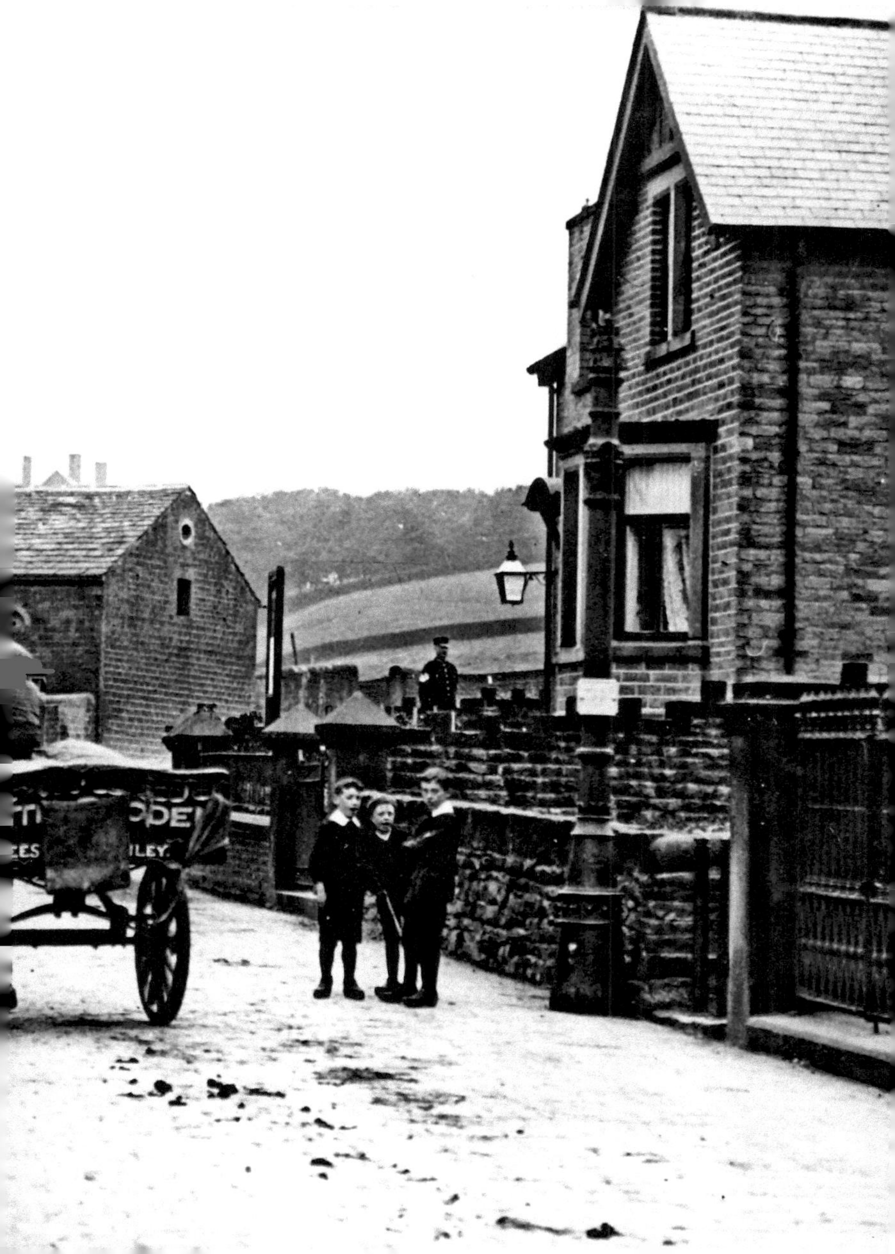

ODE
EES
ILEY.

# 4. GAS WORKS

Haworth Gas Company built their works on this site in 1857. They were acquired by the Haworth Local Board in 1871 and later rebuilt. Gas was last made here in 1954 when Haworth gas works became a distribution centre for gas piped up from Keighley. The works were finally closed in 1972 with the advent of natural gas. Our photographs show the site before and after it was cleared to make a car park.

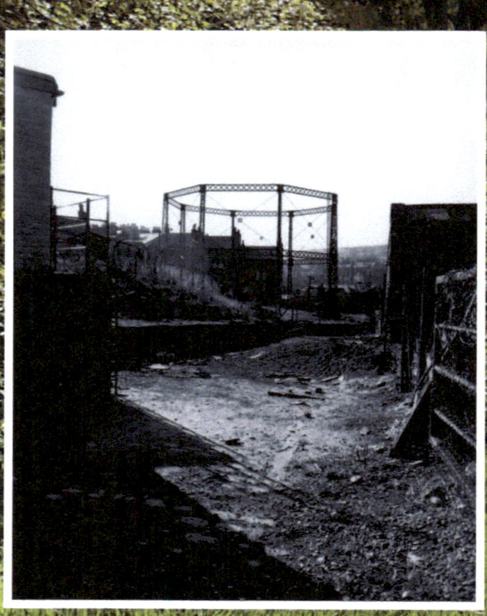

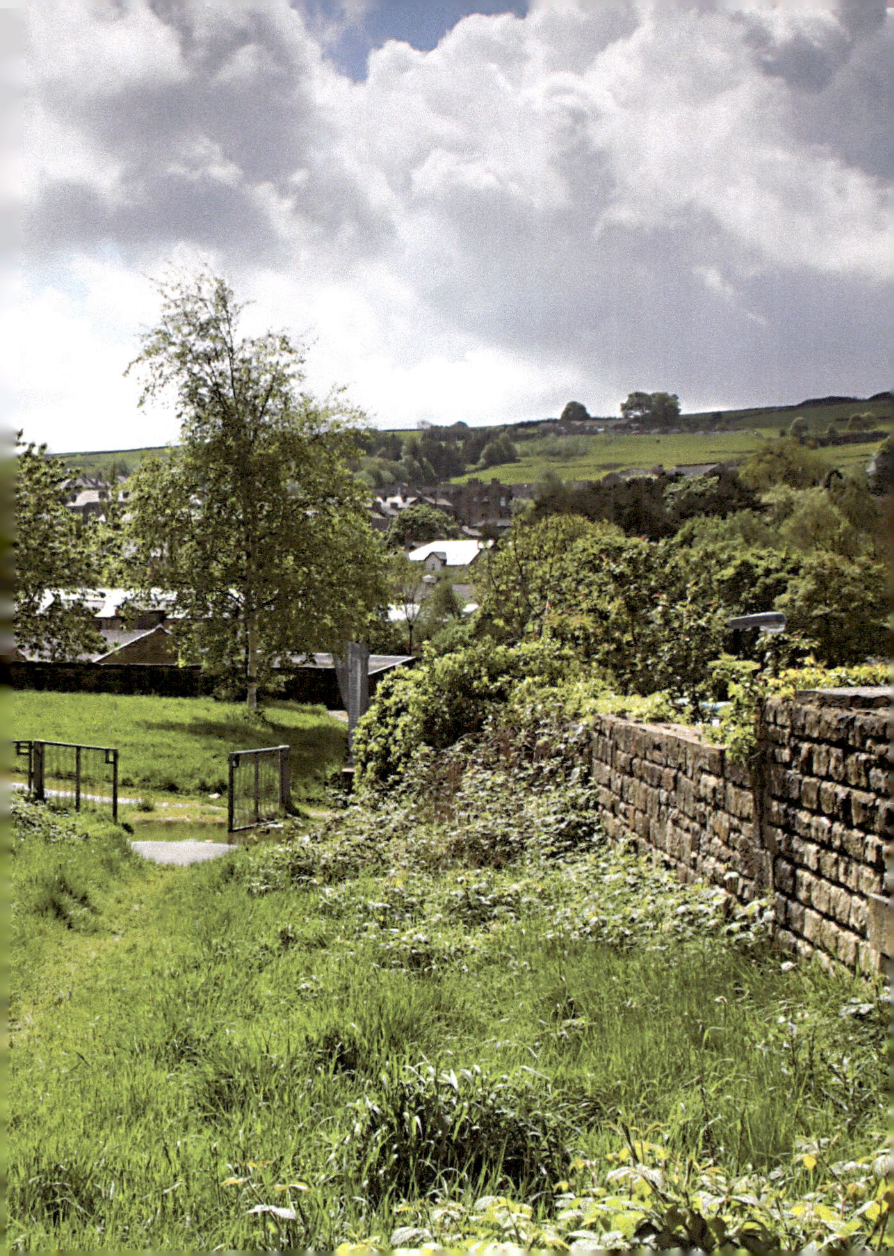

# 5. MILL HEY

A view along Mill Hey from the top of River Street to the railway station shows a dozen or so shops serving Haworth Brow. In this photograph there were a grocer, butcher, printer, provision merchant, furniture dealer, fruiterer, two tailors, a chemist, a dairyman and a confectioner. Mill Hey is still better provided with useful shops for residents than any other part of Haworth.

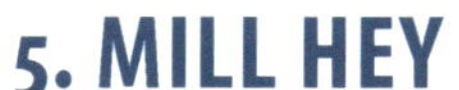

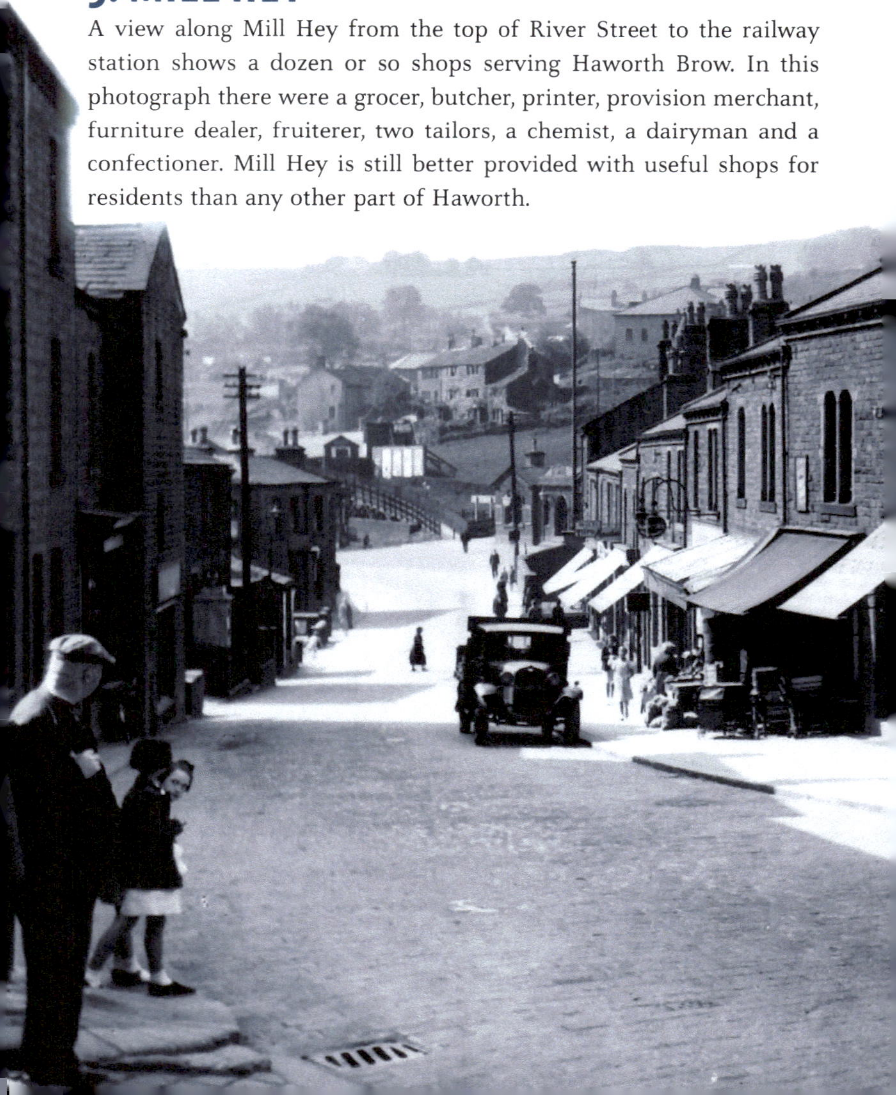

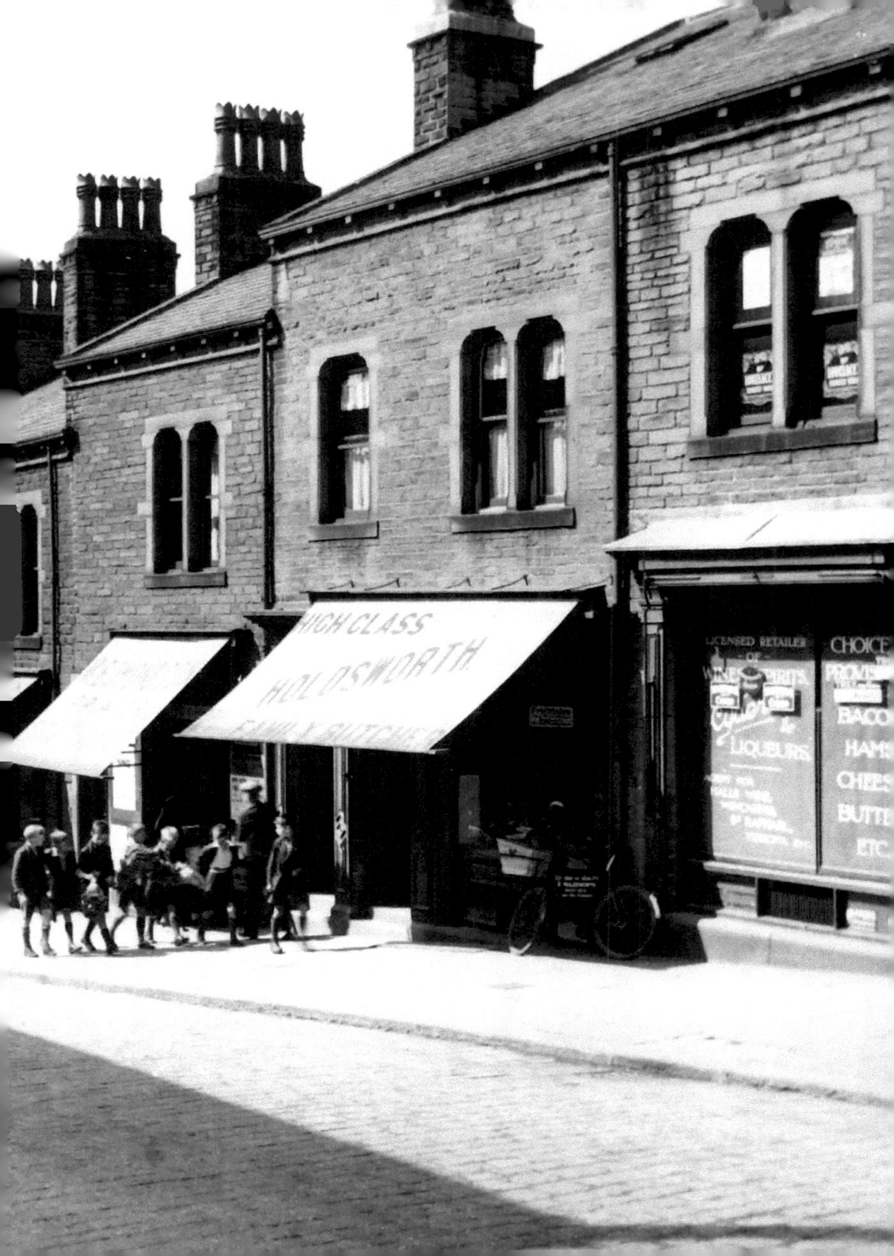

HIGH CLASS
HOLDSWORTH
FAMILY BUTCHER
LICENSED RETAILER
OF
WINES SPIRITS
&
LIQUEURS
CHOICE
BACON
HAMS
CHEESE
BUTTER
ETC

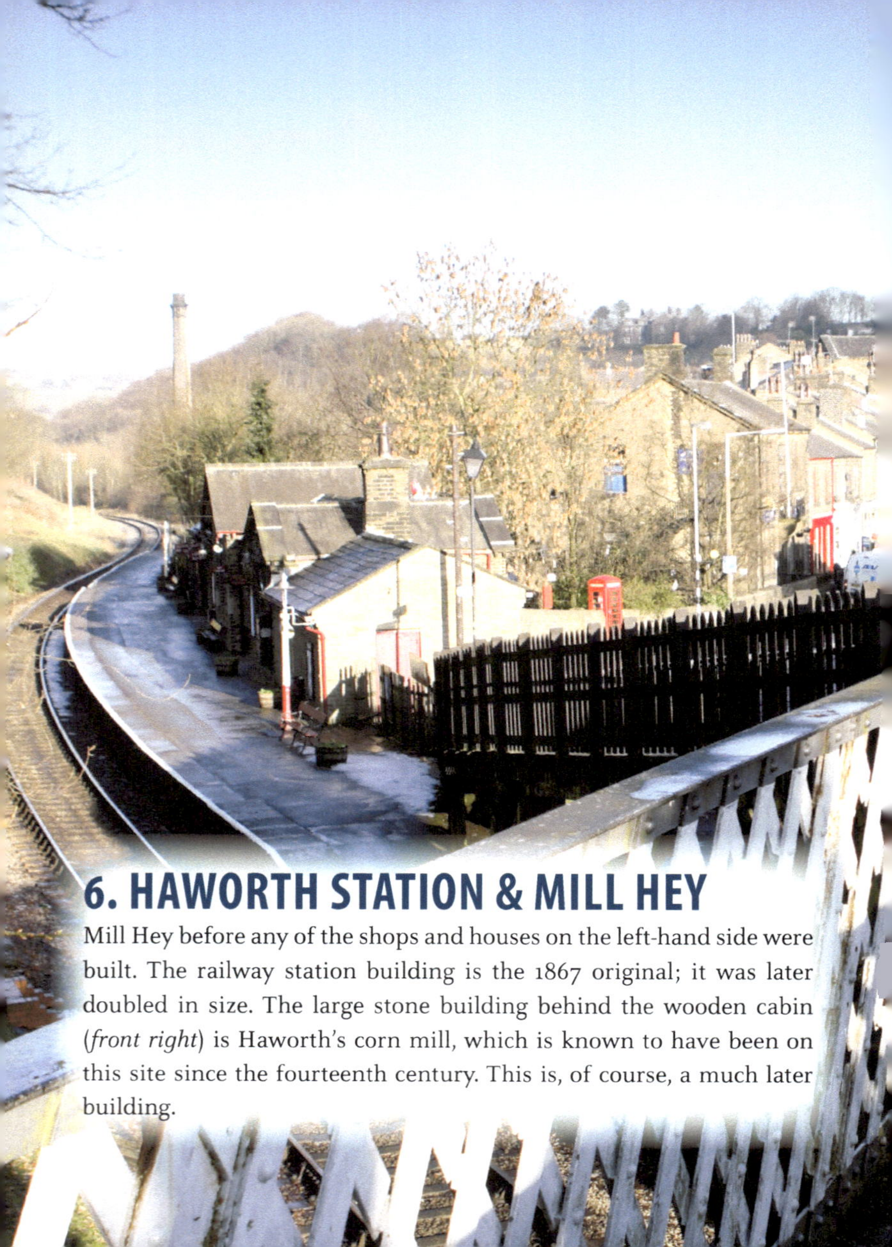

# 6. HAWORTH STATION & MILL HEY

Mill Hey before any of the shops and houses on the left-hand side were built. The railway station building is the 1867 original; it was later doubled in size. The large stone building behind the wooden cabin (*front right*) is Haworth's corn mill, which is known to have been on this site since the fourteenth century. This is, of course, a much later building.

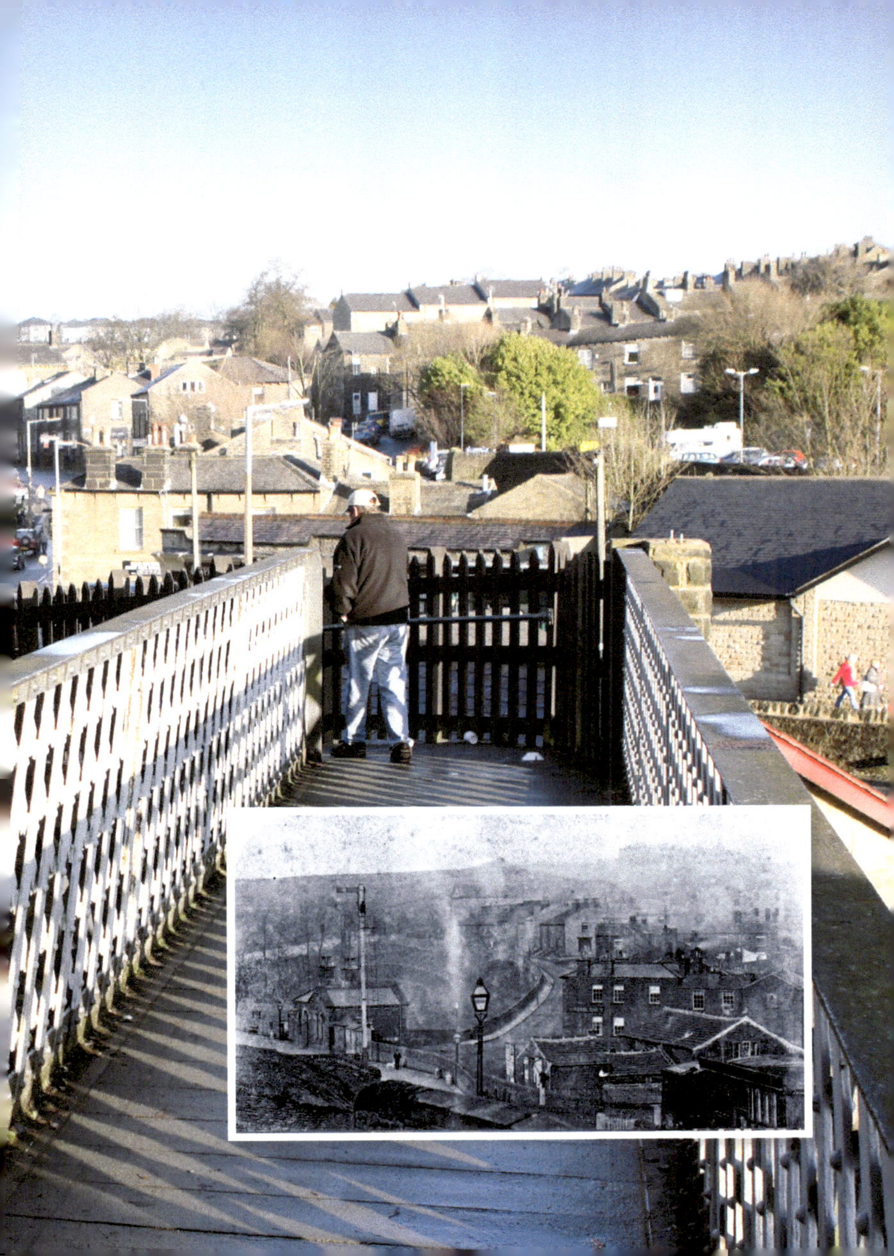

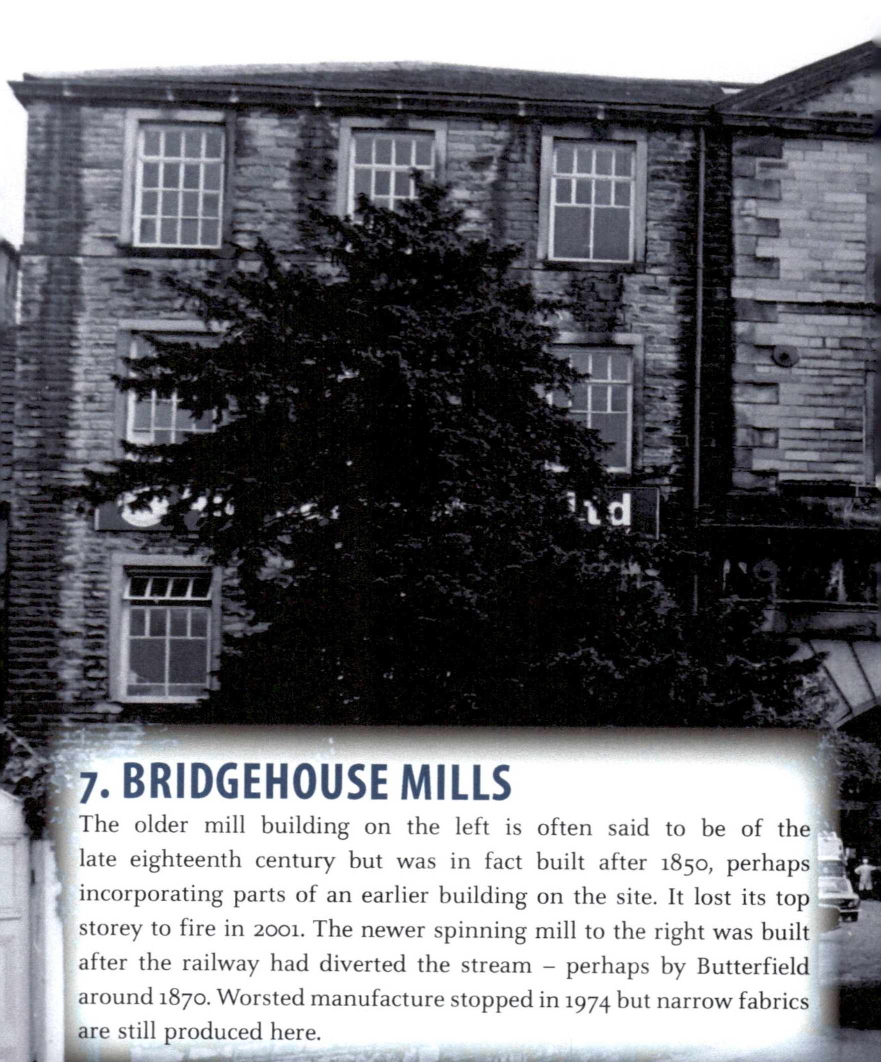

# 7. BRIDGEHOUSE MILLS

The older mill building on the left is often said to be of the late eighteenth century but was in fact built after 1850, perhaps incorporating parts of an earlier building on the site. It lost its top storey to fire in 2001. The newer spinning mill to the right was built after the railway had diverted the stream – perhaps by Butterfield around 1870. Worsted manufacture stopped in 1974 but narrow fabrics are still produced here.

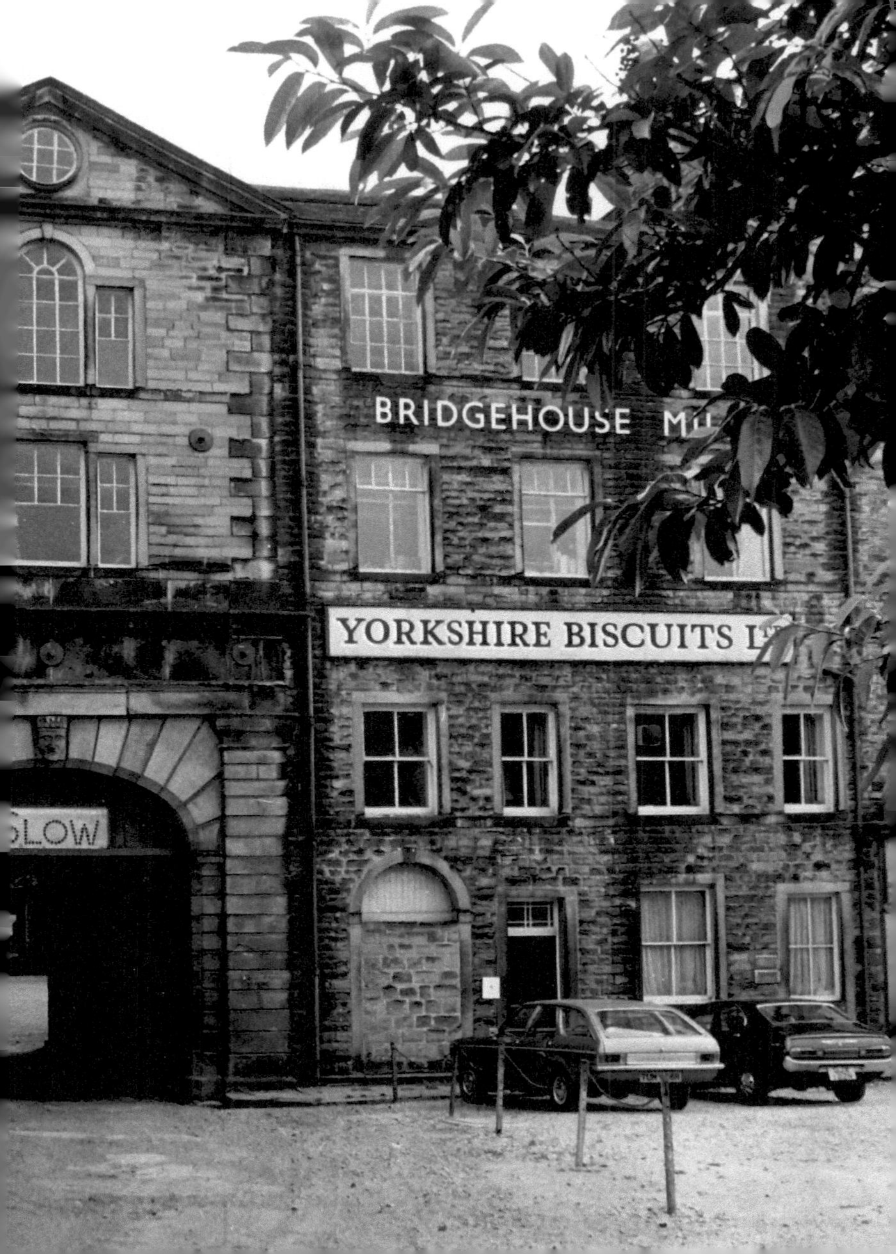

BRIDGEHOUSE MI
YORKSHIRE BISCUITS L
LOW

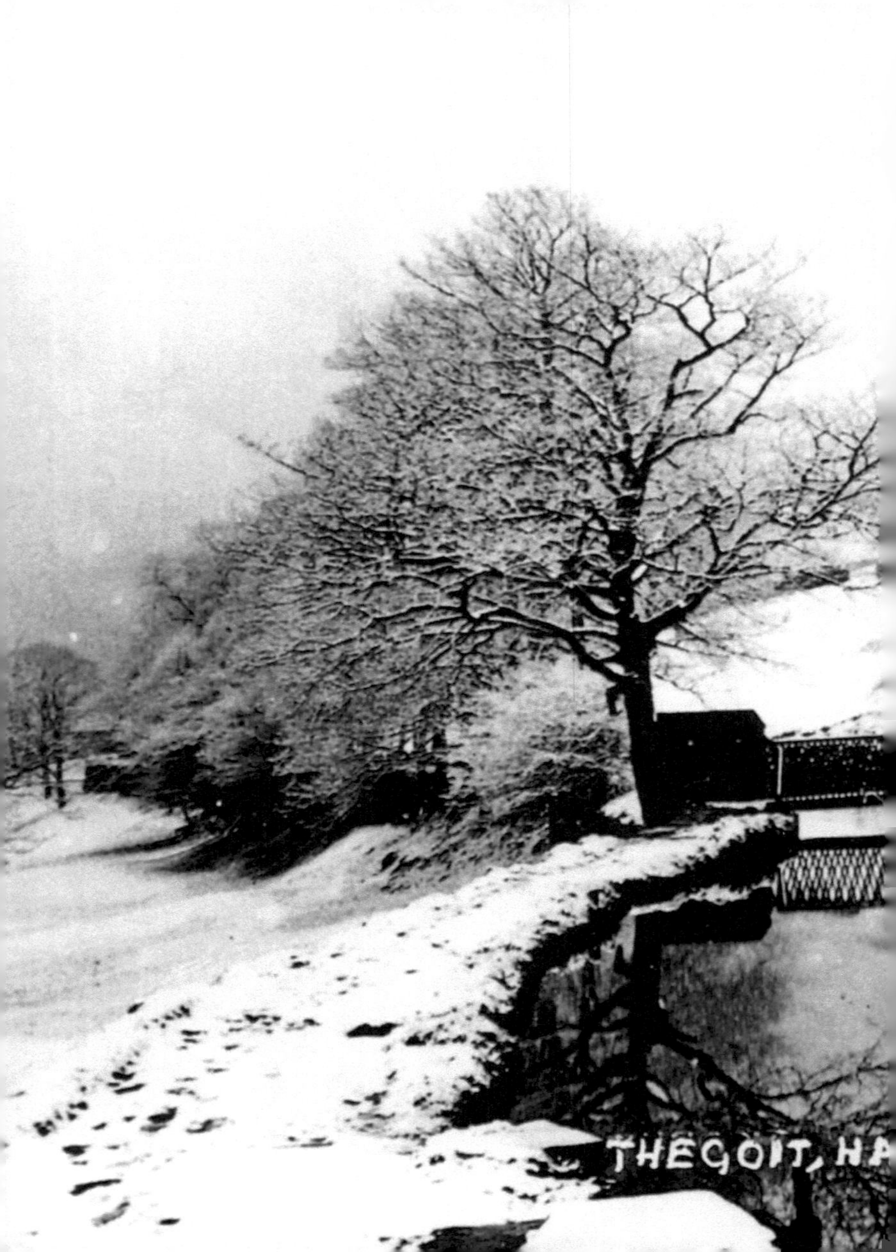
THE GOIT, HA

# 8. BRIDGEHOUSE MILL GOIT

Bridgehouse Mill was water powered for much of its history and a large water wheel survived, as a supplement to steam power, into the early twentieth century. To provide water for the wheel, this half-mile-long goit was constructed around 1811. It runs through picturesque farmland in the valley of the Bridgehouse Beck and became a popular place of resort. It was a favourite subject for photographers who sometimes captioned their cards 'Bonny Goit Side'.

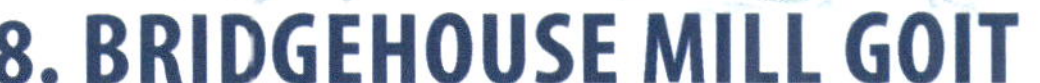

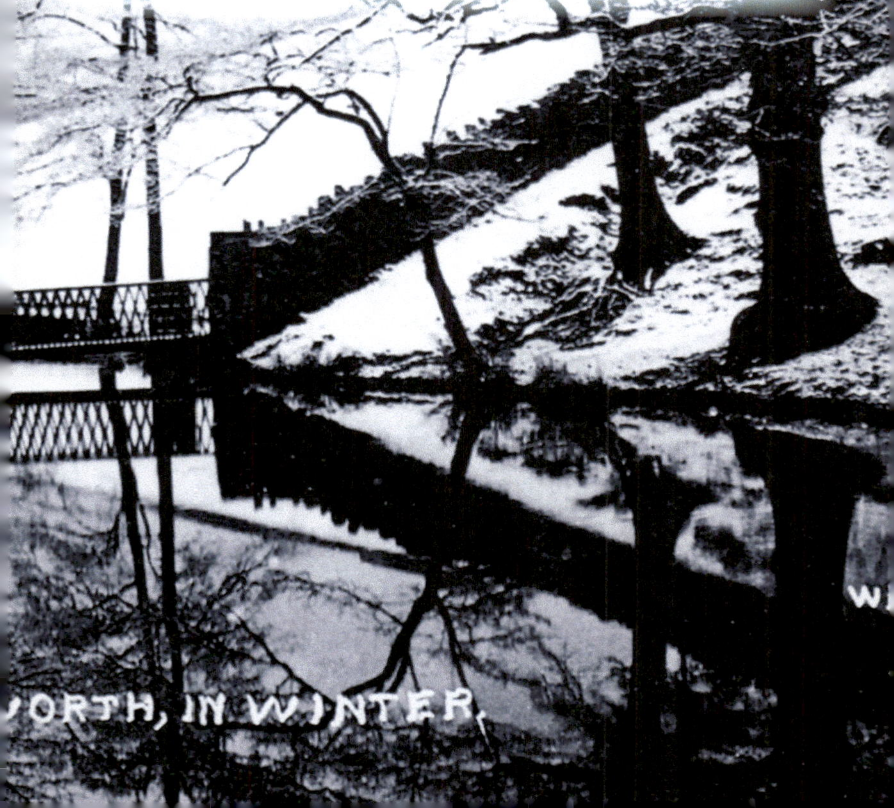

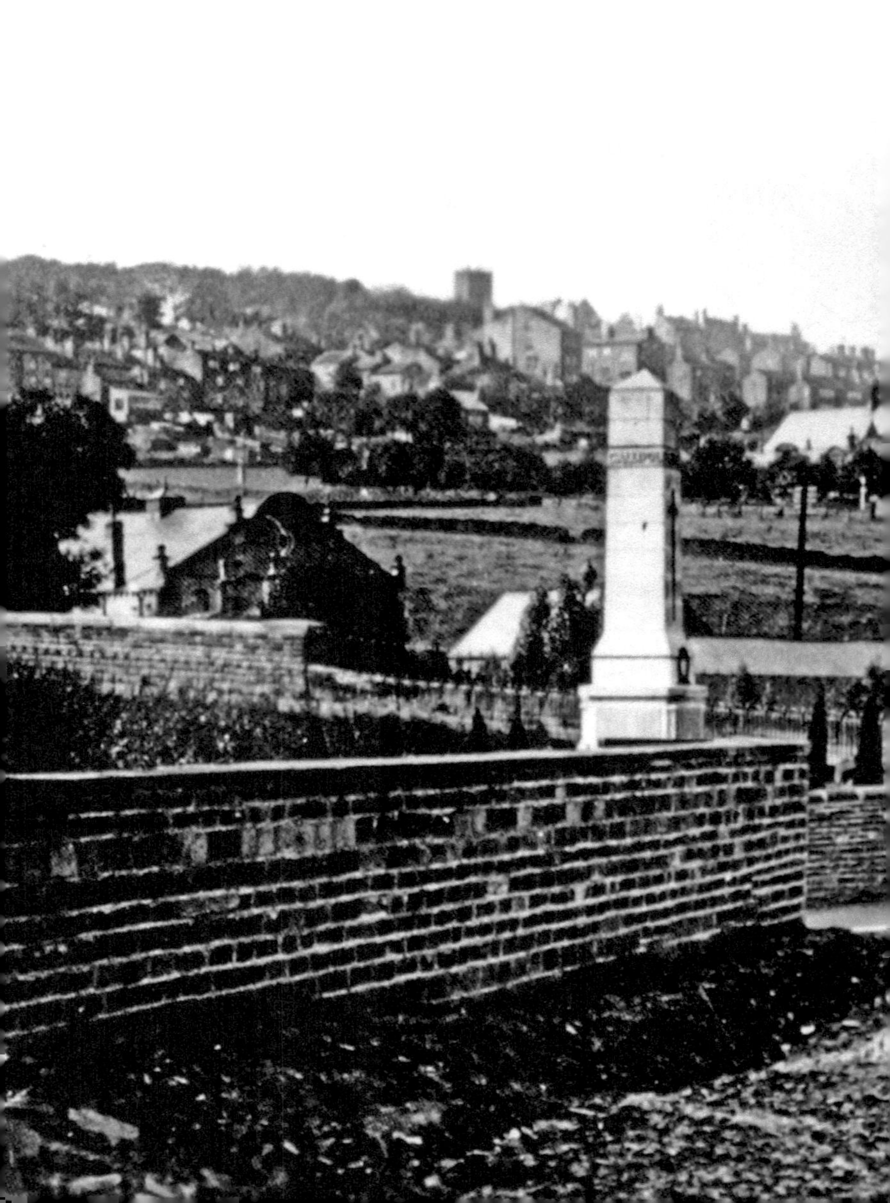

# 9. BRIDGEHOUSE & HAWORTH WAR MEMORIAL

Haworth's War Memorial was dedicated in 1923 and this picture was taken not many years after. Across the fields, which now form part of the park, can be seen the Board School buildings and the very new looking Haworth Institute of 1924. This was the successor to the old Haworth Mechanics' Institute, which closed around this time.

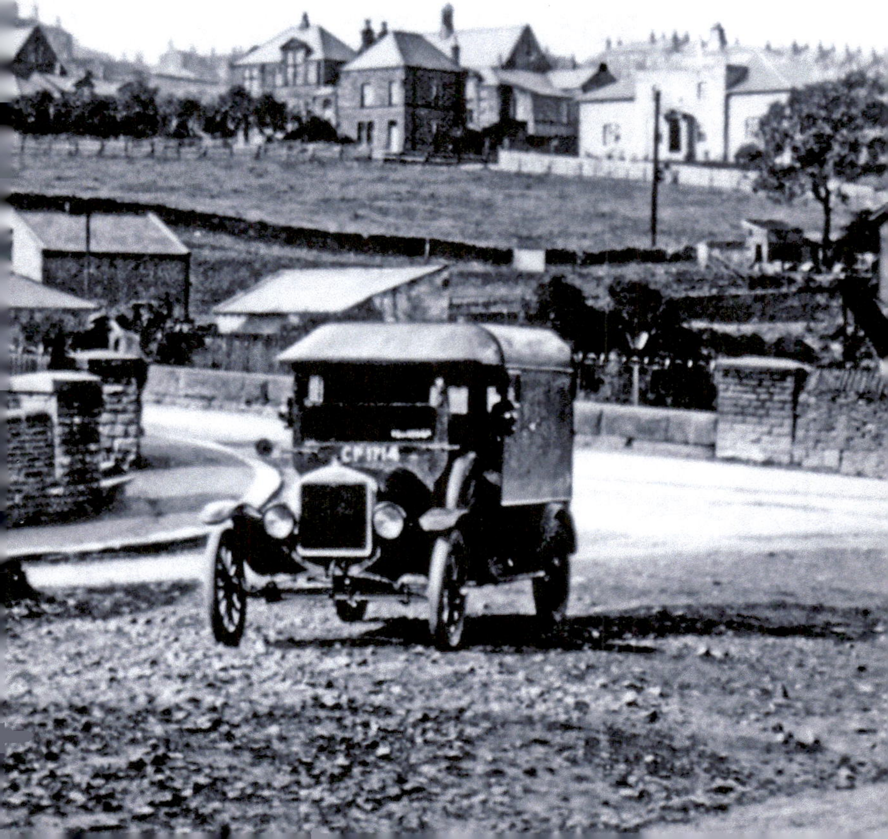

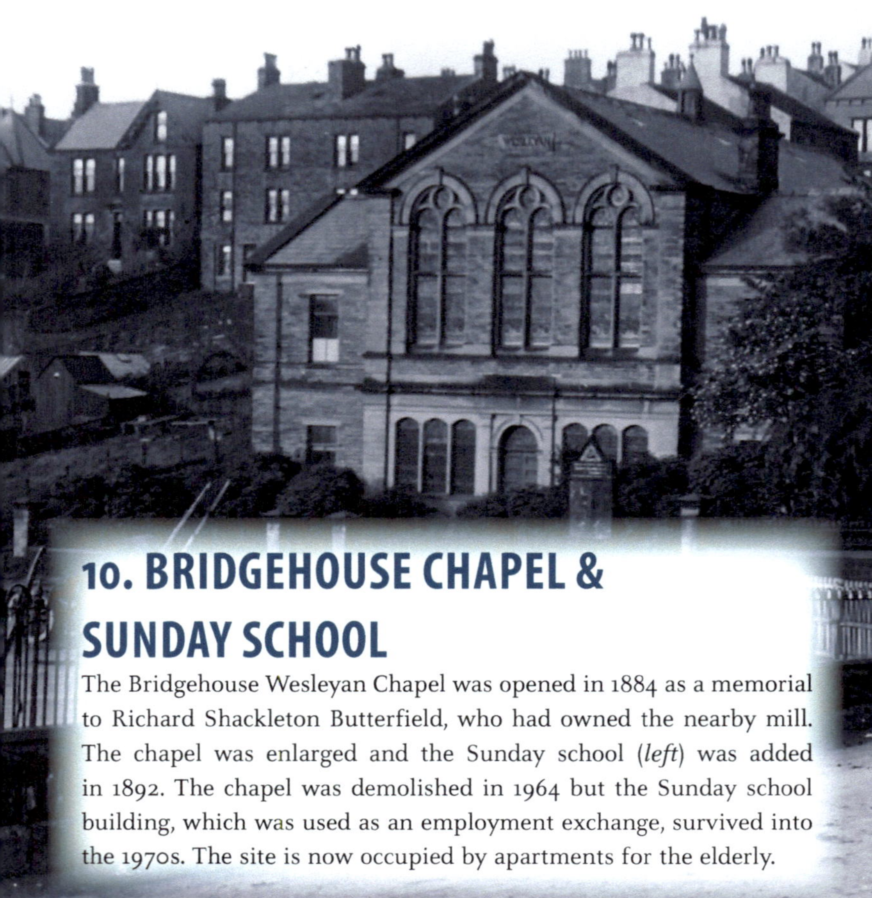

# 10. BRIDGEHOUSE CHAPEL & SUNDAY SCHOOL

The Bridgehouse Wesleyan Chapel was opened in 1884 as a memorial to Richard Shackleton Butterfield, who had owned the nearby mill. The chapel was enlarged and the Sunday school (*left*) was added in 1892. The chapel was demolished in 1964 but the Sunday school building, which was used as an employment exchange, survived into the 1970s. The site is now occupied by apartments for the elderly.

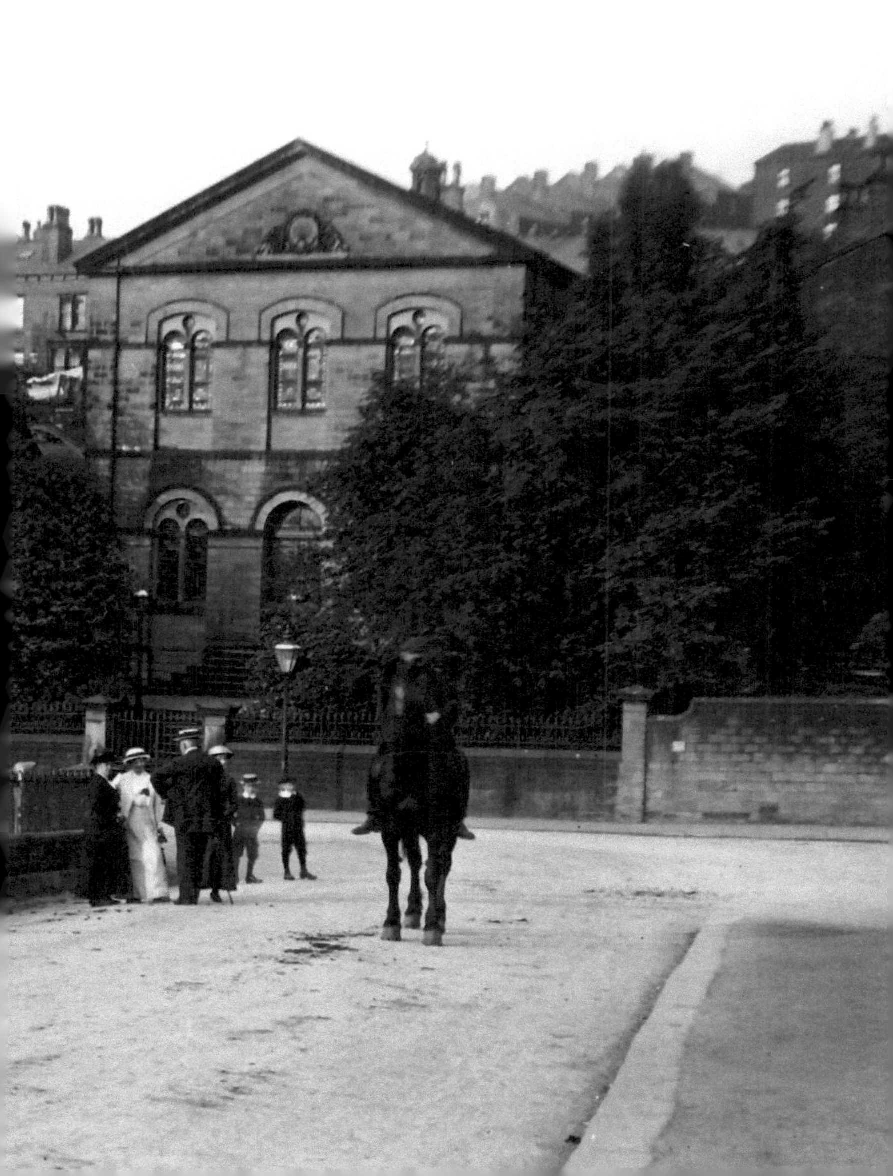

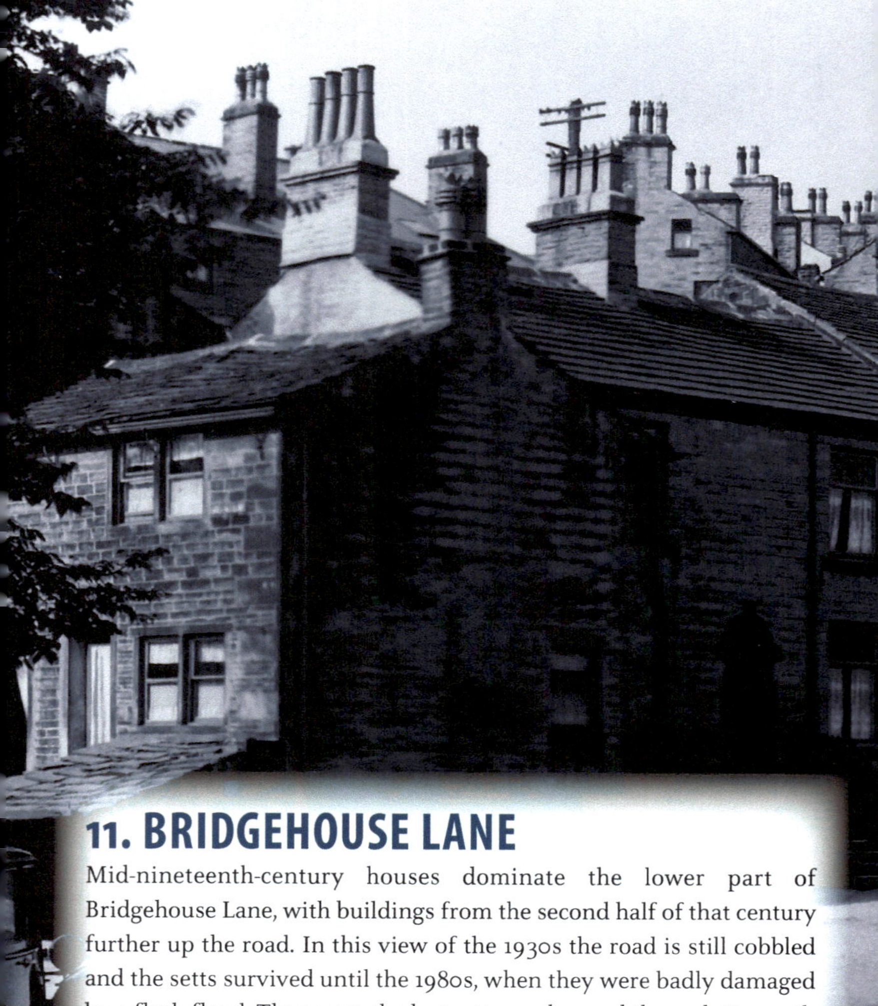

# 11. BRIDGEHOUSE LANE

Mid-nineteenth-century houses dominate the lower part of Bridgehouse Lane, with buildings from the second half of that century further up the road. In this view of the 1930s the road is still cobbled and the setts survived until the 1980s, when they were badly damaged by a flash flood. They were the last setts on the road through Haworth towards Colne and the chance to surface the road with tarmacadam was taken.

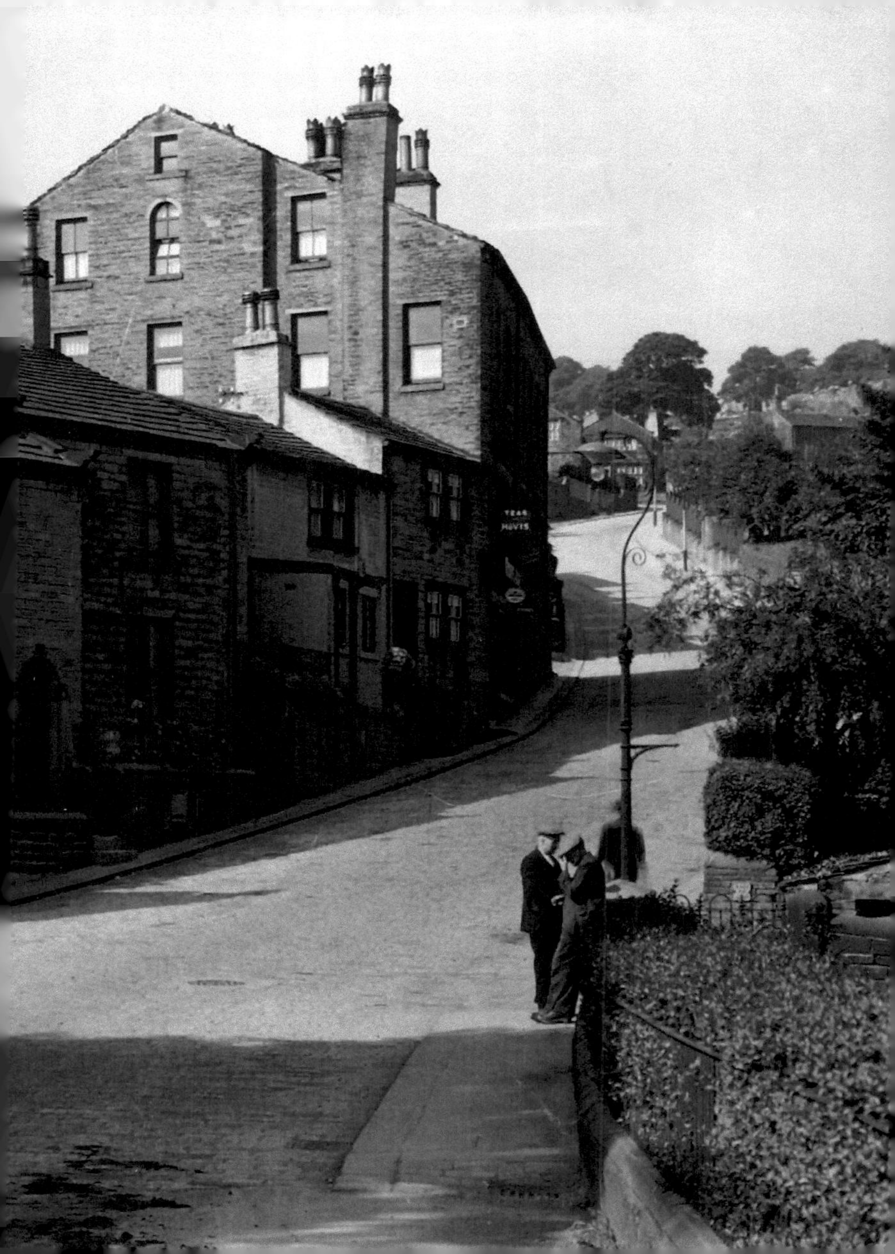

# 12. HIPPODROME CINEMA

The Hippodrome was Haworth's first cinema and it opened in 1913. After the Brontë Cinema opened on the Brow in the early twenties, the Hippodrome was always referred to as 't'owd 'uns' – the more recent cinema, naturally, being called 't'new 'uns'. The last film, *Trooper Hook*, was shown in 1961. After that the building was used as a bingo hall, then as a 'Bygone Days' museum. It has now been converted into apartments.

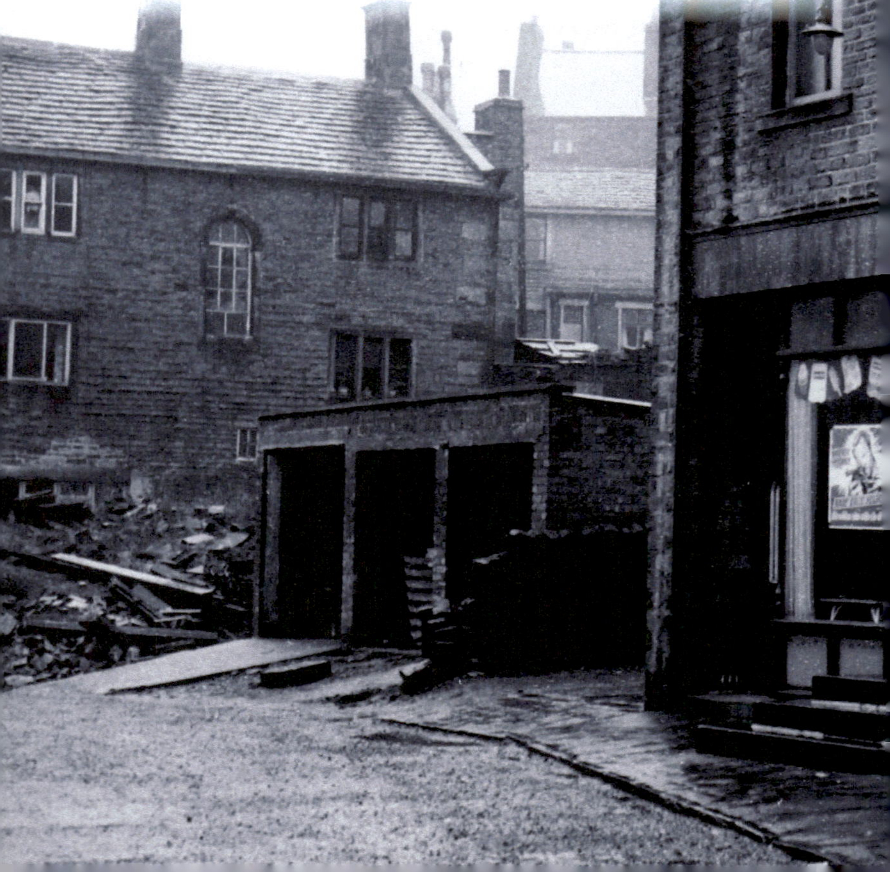

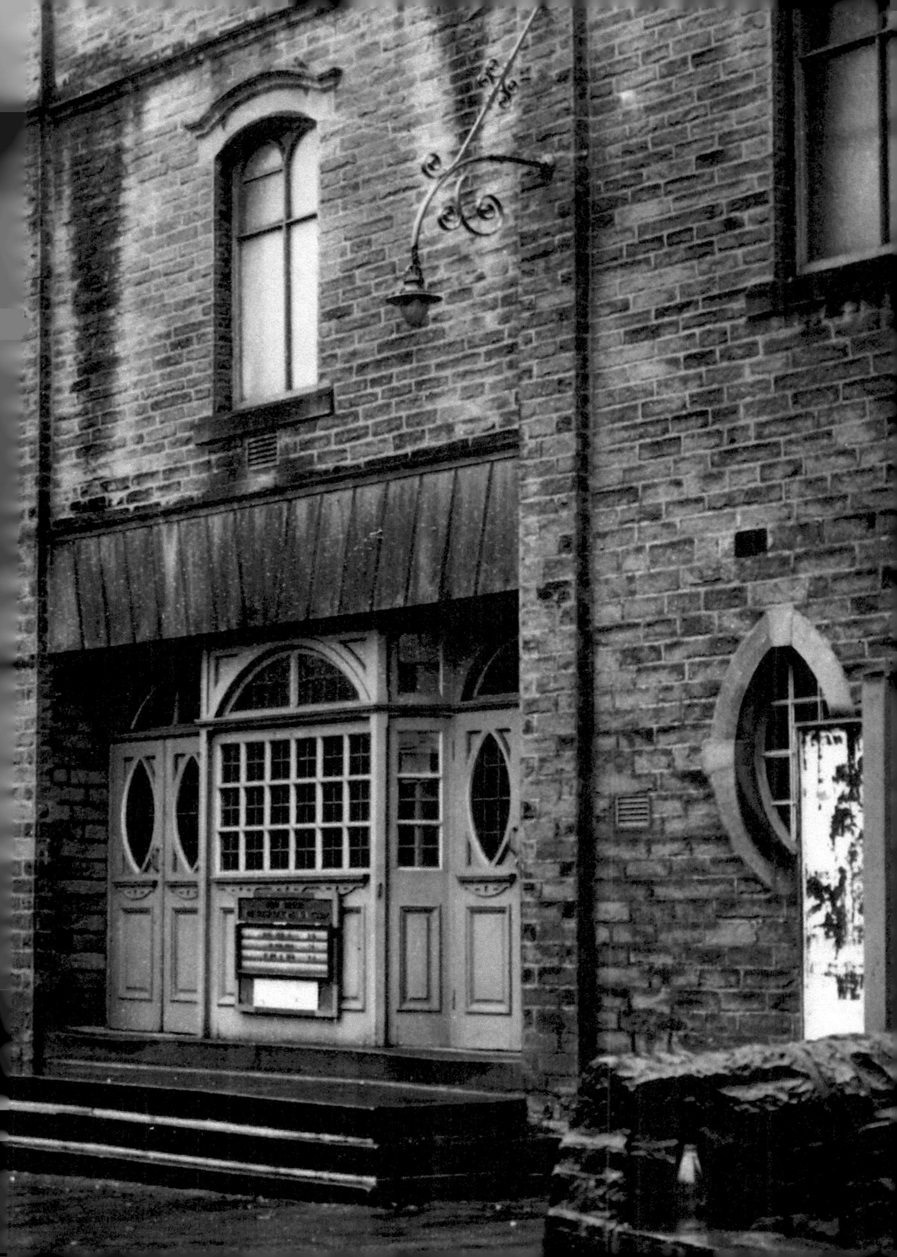

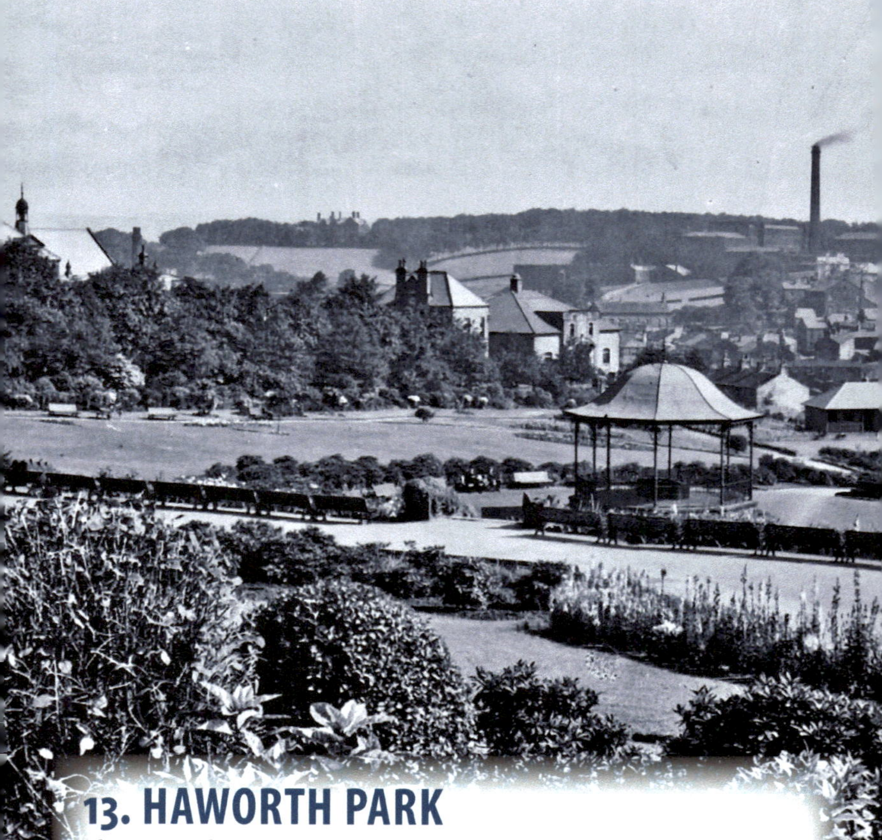

## 13. HAWORTH PARK

This general view across Haworth Central Park, opened in 1929, also includes the bowling green, which commemorates the Coronation of George VI in 1937. The mill chimney in the distance belonged to Lees Syke Mill, which has now been largely demolished to make way for houses.

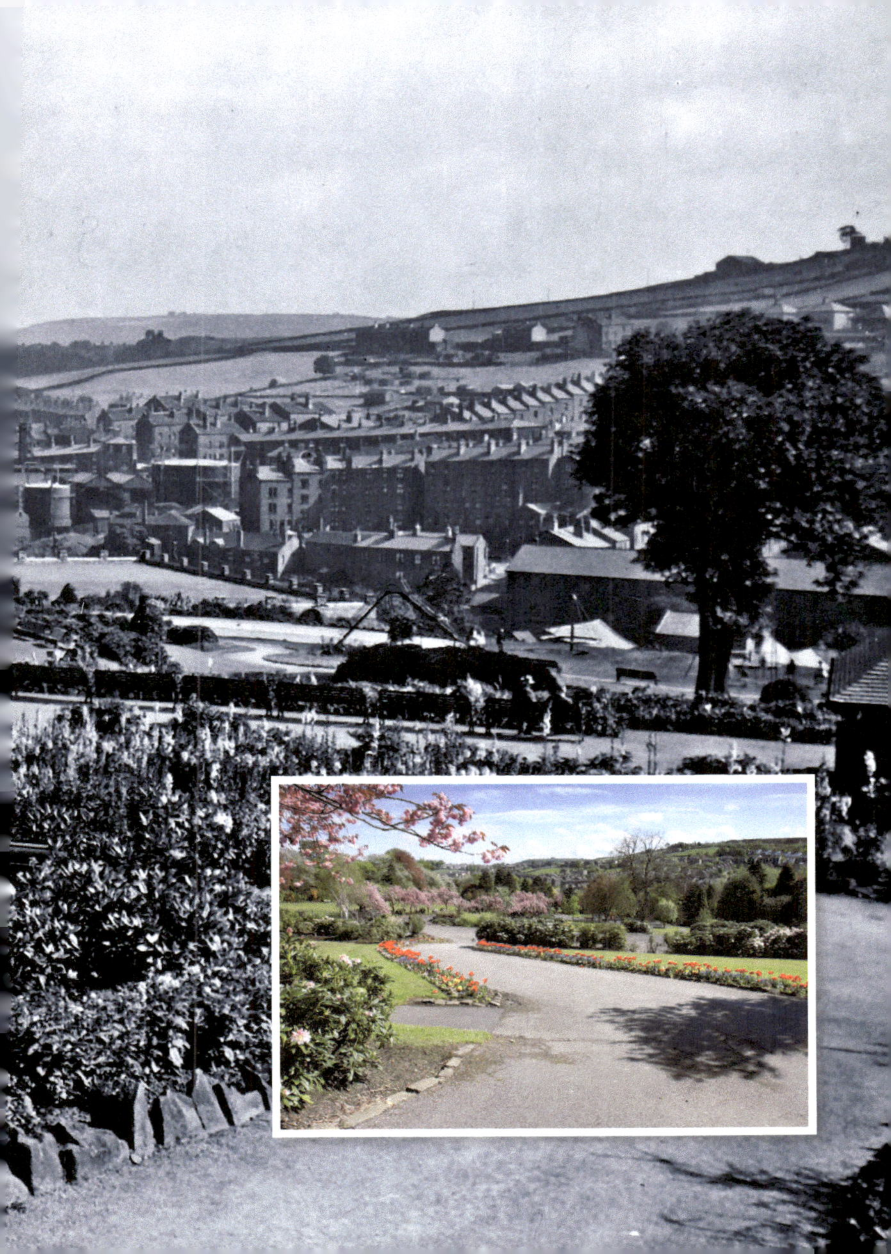

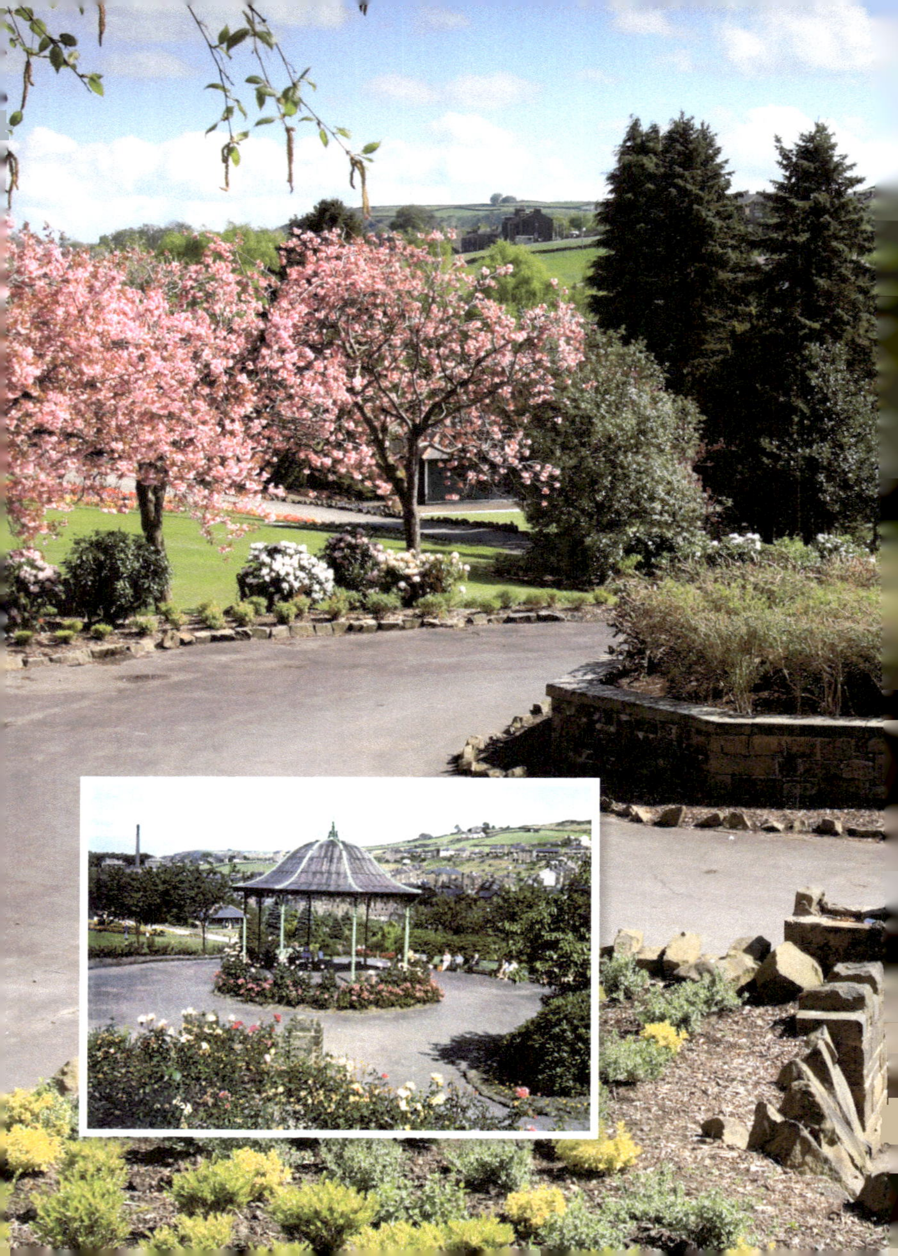

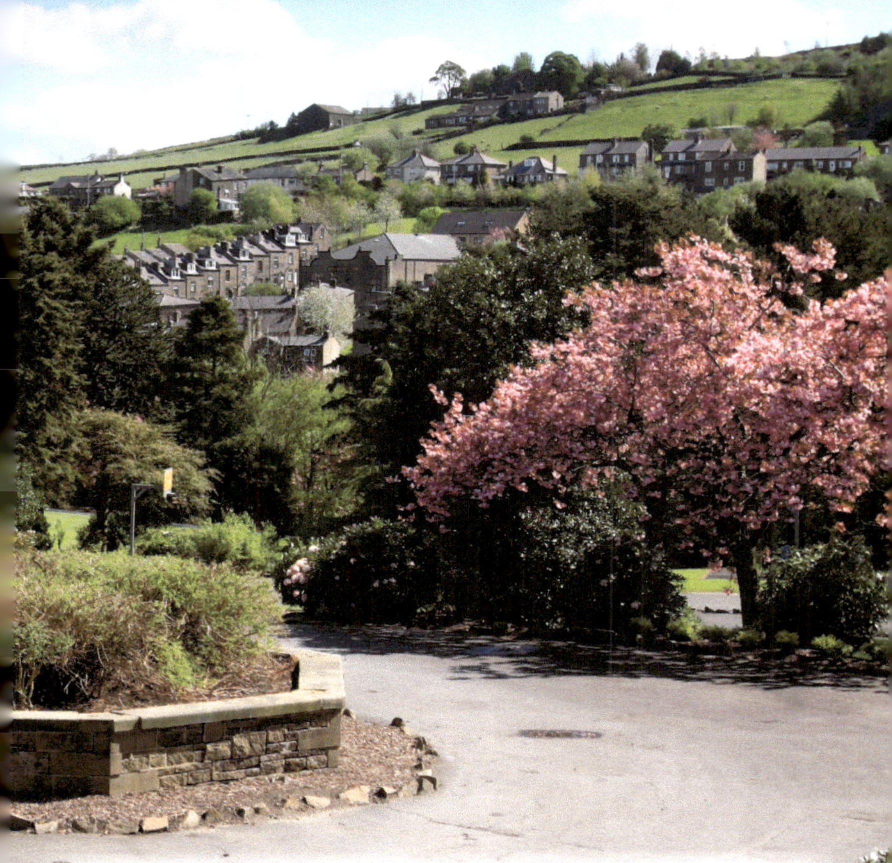

# 14. HAWORTH PARK, BANDSTAND

The bandstand was a central feature of the park for decades, seeing regular performances by the Haworth Band, which dates back to the 1860s. It was also used for local events such as the crowning of the Gala Queen. The bandstand was removed many years ago but, thanks to the efforts of the Friends of Haworth Park, a new bandstand is now in place.

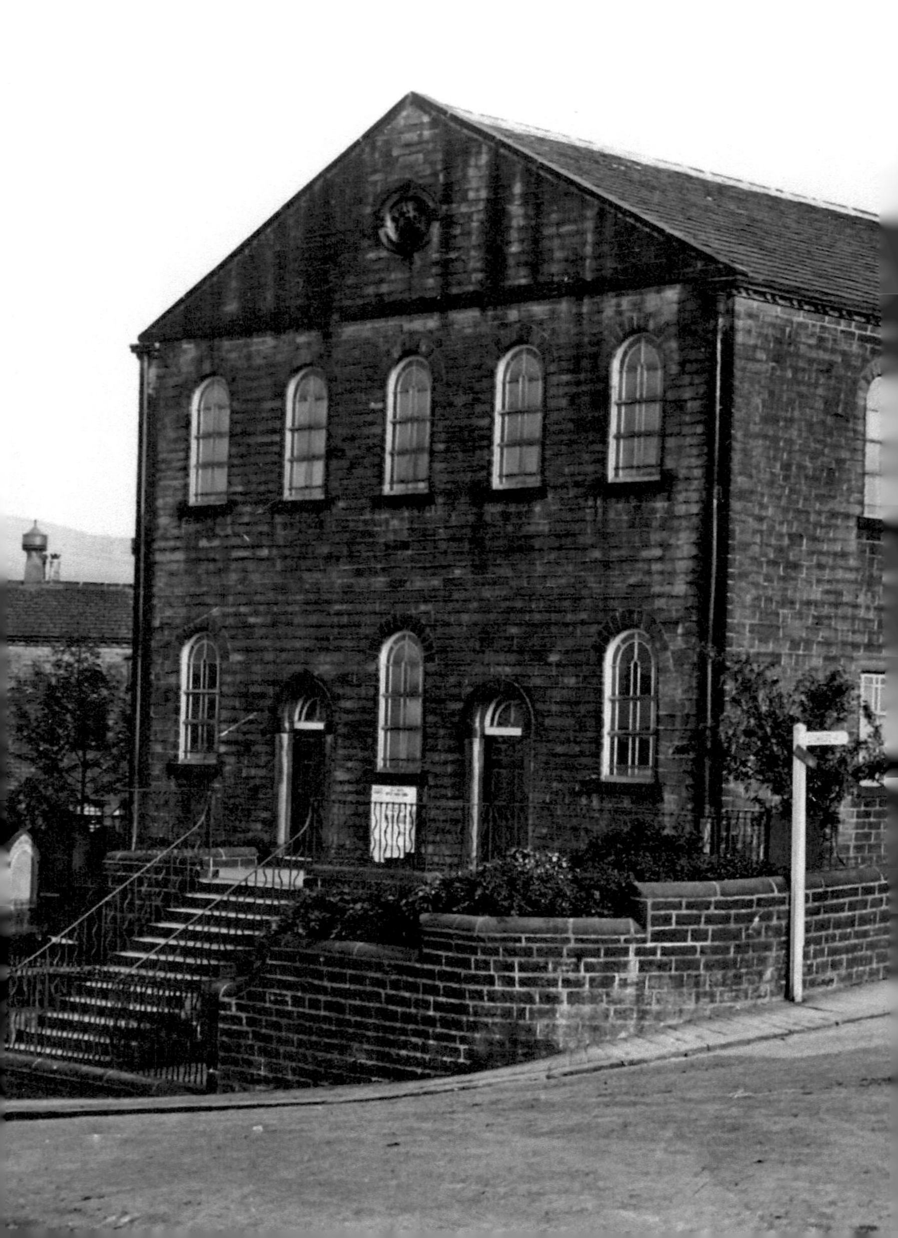

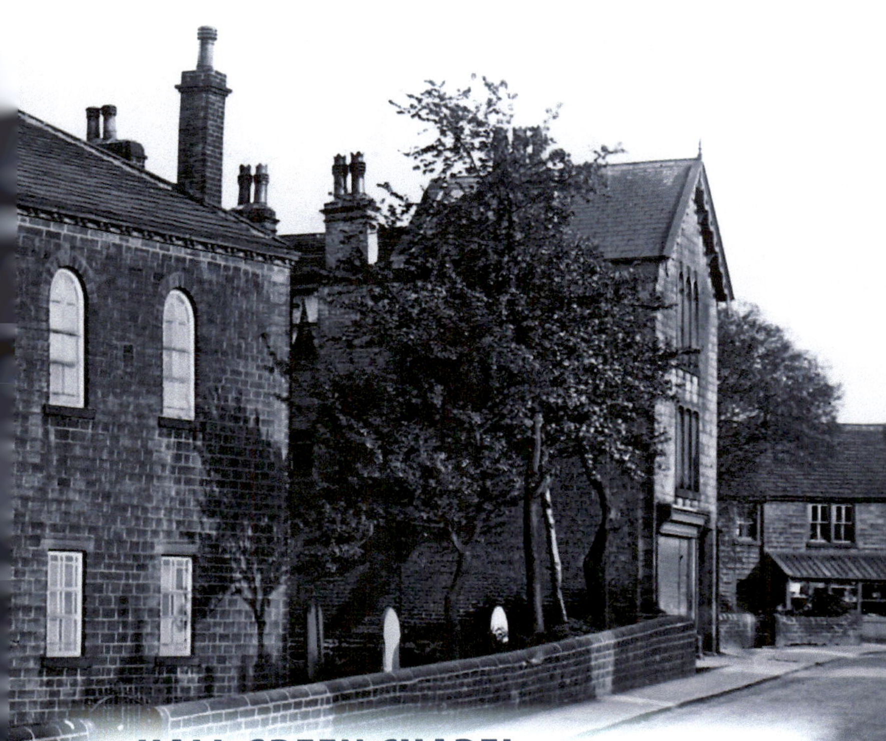

# 15. HALL GREEN CHAPEL

Hall Green Baptist Chapel is the oldest surviving place of worship in Haworth, having been built in 1824. It had its origins in a secession from the West Lane Baptist Chapel over music some years before. Visible in the distance (*extreme right*) is Sun Street Stores, which was started as a grocery shop by Tobias Lambert almost 200 years ago and is still fulfilling the same function today.

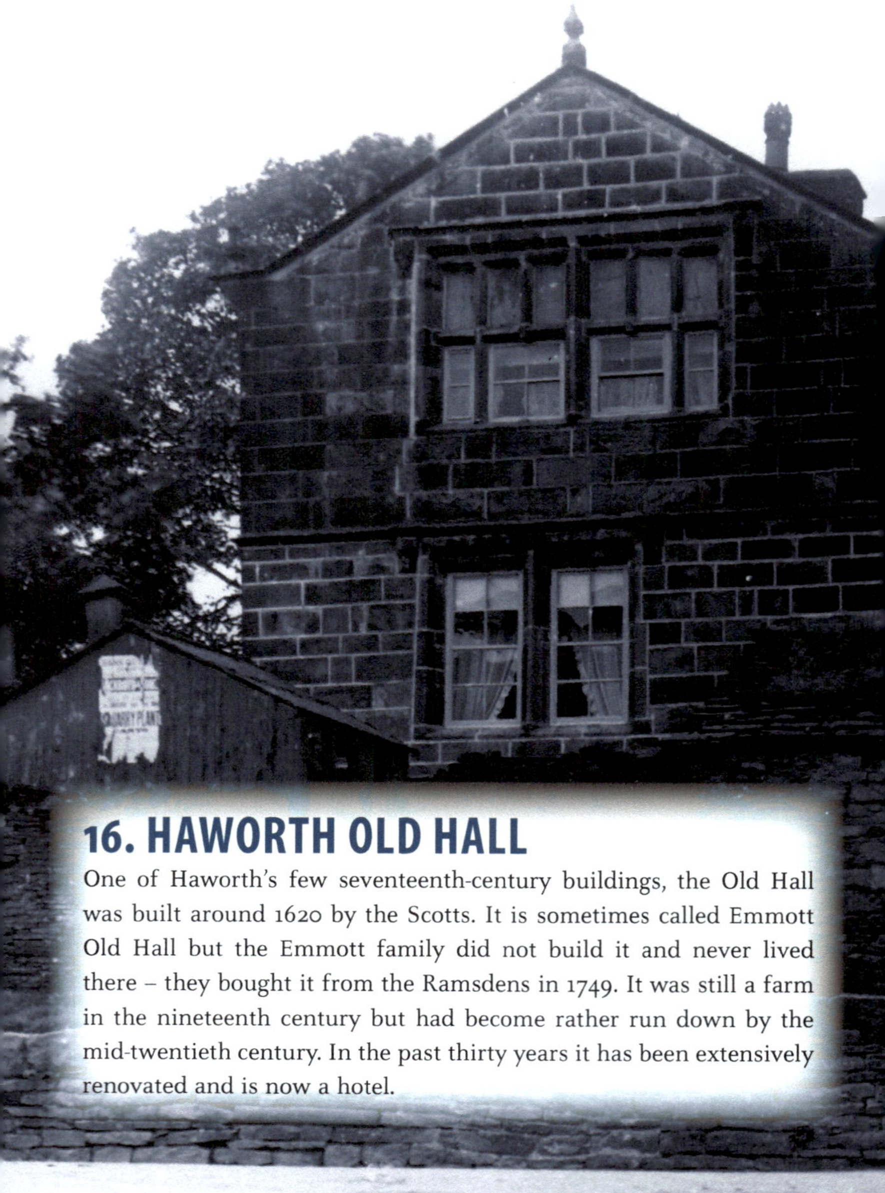

# 16. HAWORTH OLD HALL

One of Haworth's few seventeenth-century buildings, the Old Hall was built around 1620 by the Scotts. It is sometimes called Emmott Old Hall but the Emmott family did not build it and never lived there – they bought it from the Ramsdens in 1749. It was still a farm in the nineteenth century but had become rather run down by the mid-twentieth century. In the past thirty years it has been extensively renovated and is now a hotel.

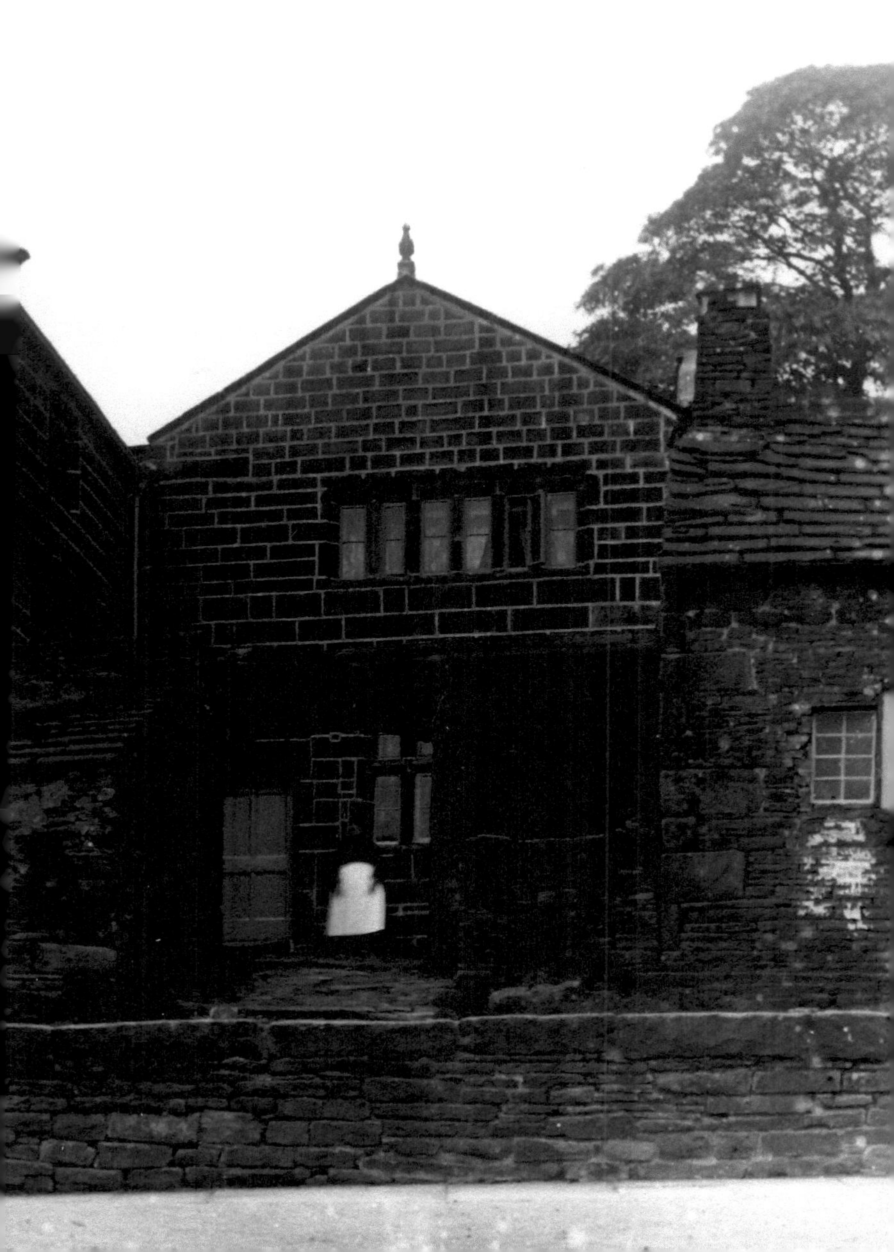

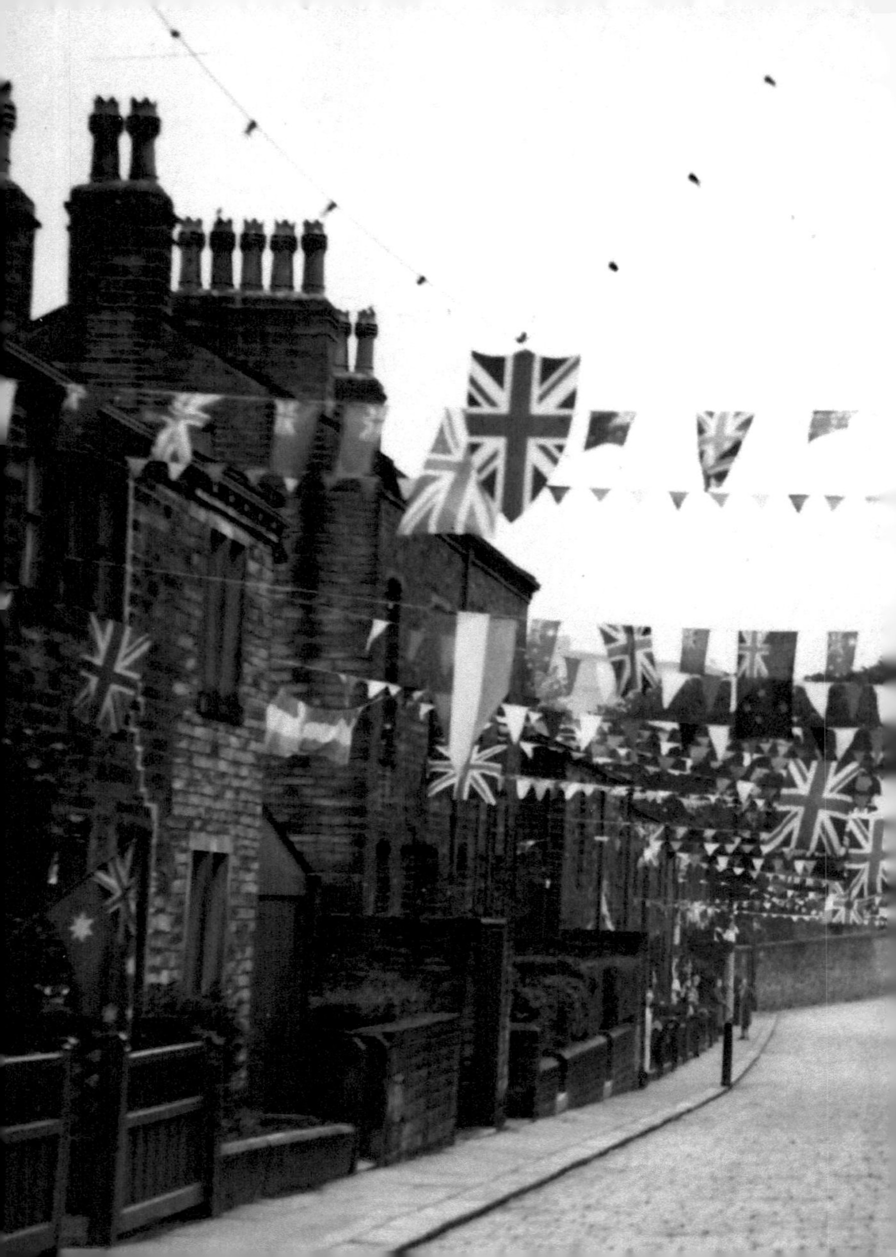

# 17. SUN STREET, VE DAY CELEBRATIONS

Here we see Sun Street profusely decorated with the Union flag and the flags of the Allies for VE day. The photographer has captured a view looking towards Oxenhope with nineteenth-century houses on either side of the road. Notice that the road is still cobbled.

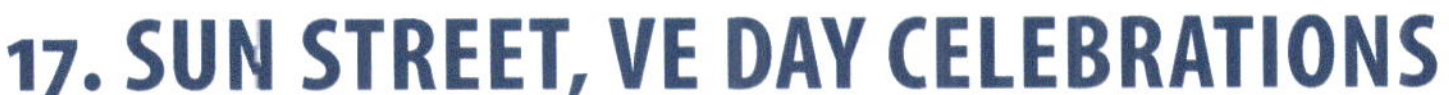

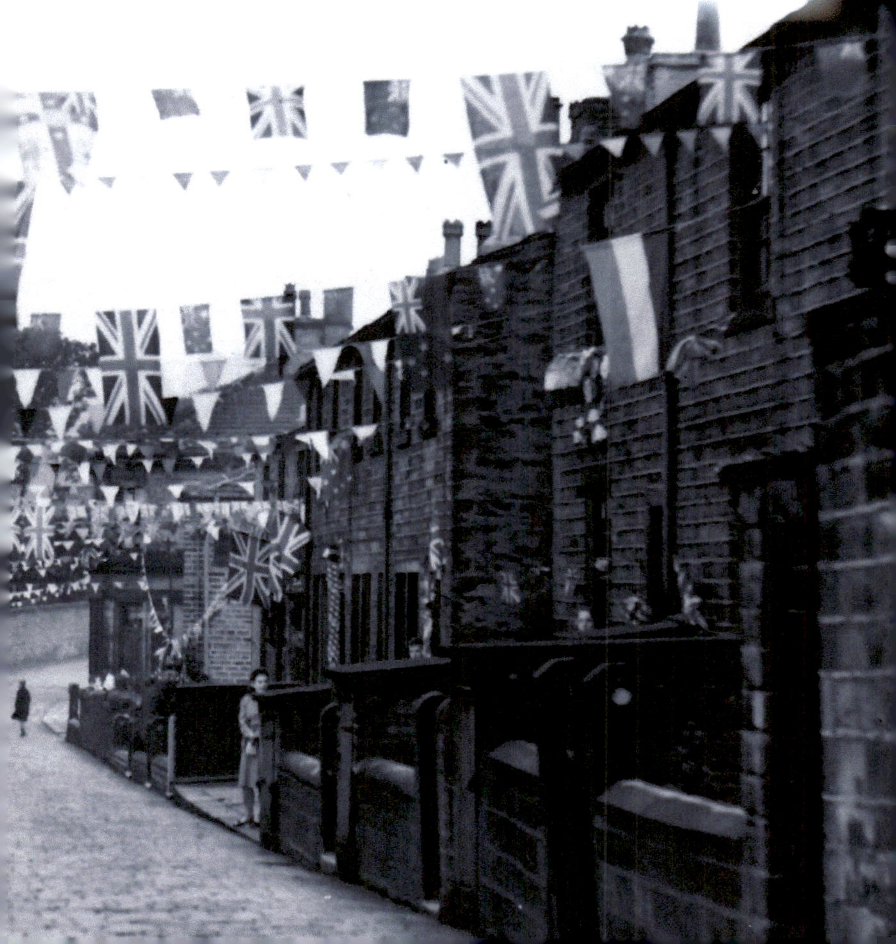

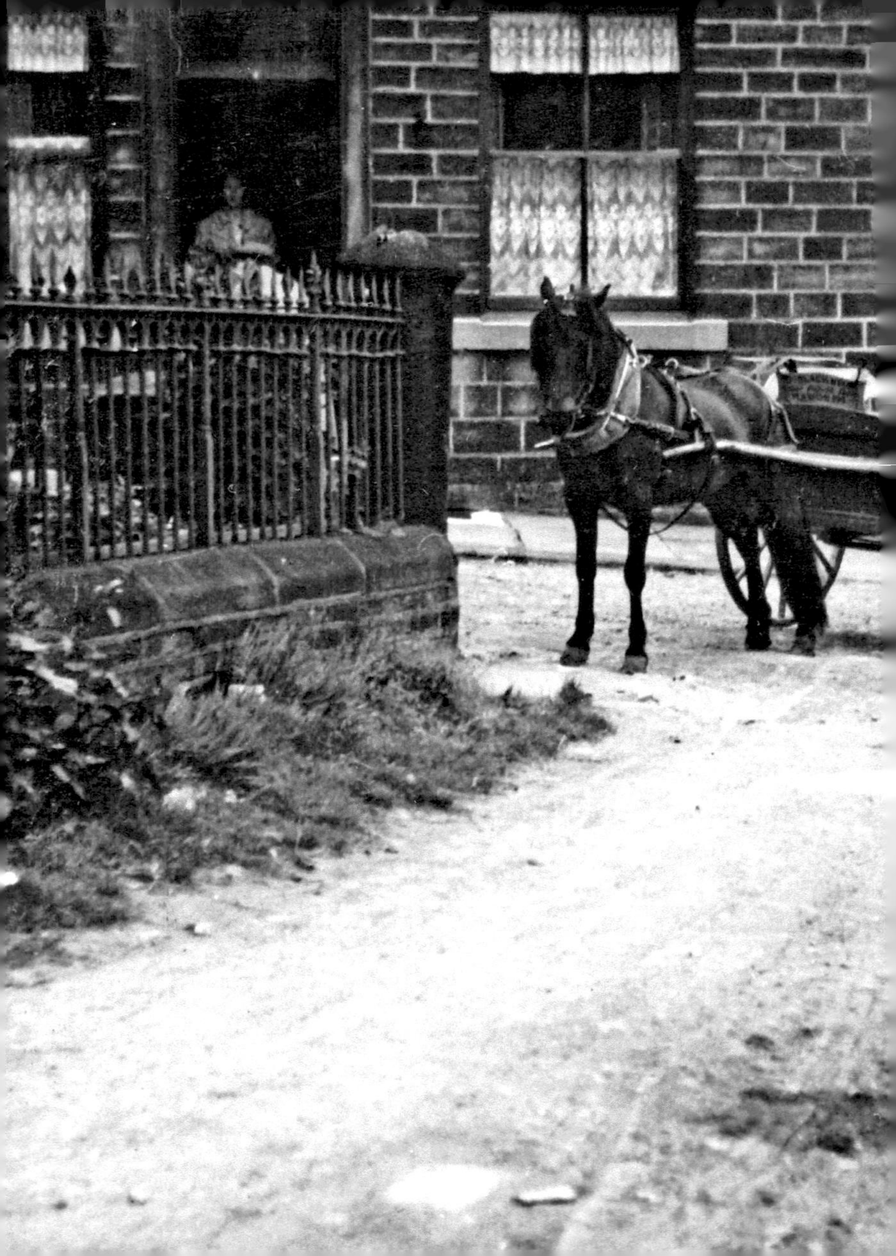

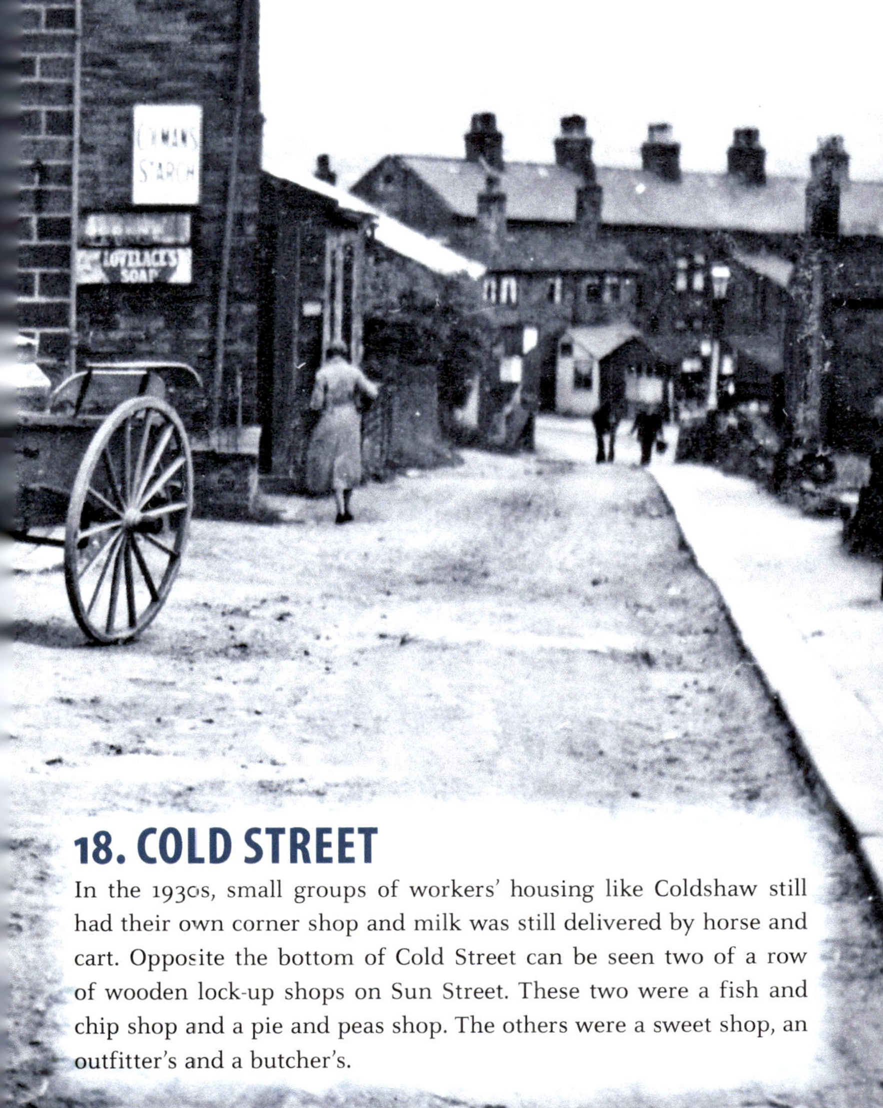


# 18. COLD STREET

In the 1930s, small groups of workers' housing like Coldshaw still had their own corner shop and milk was still delivered by horse and cart. Opposite the bottom of Cold Street can be seen two of a row of wooden lock-up shops on Sun Street. These two were a fish and chip shop and a pie and peas shop. The others were a sweet shop, an outfitter's and a butcher's.

# 19. MAIN STREET

The bottom of Main Street. The large house and office of William Henry Ogden, who was Haworth's Registrar for many years, is prominent on the right-hand side of the street; it was built in 1902. The 1897 co-op stands a full storey higher than its neighbours on the other side of the street. The church is clearly visible at the top of the street.

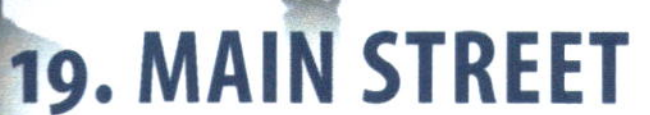

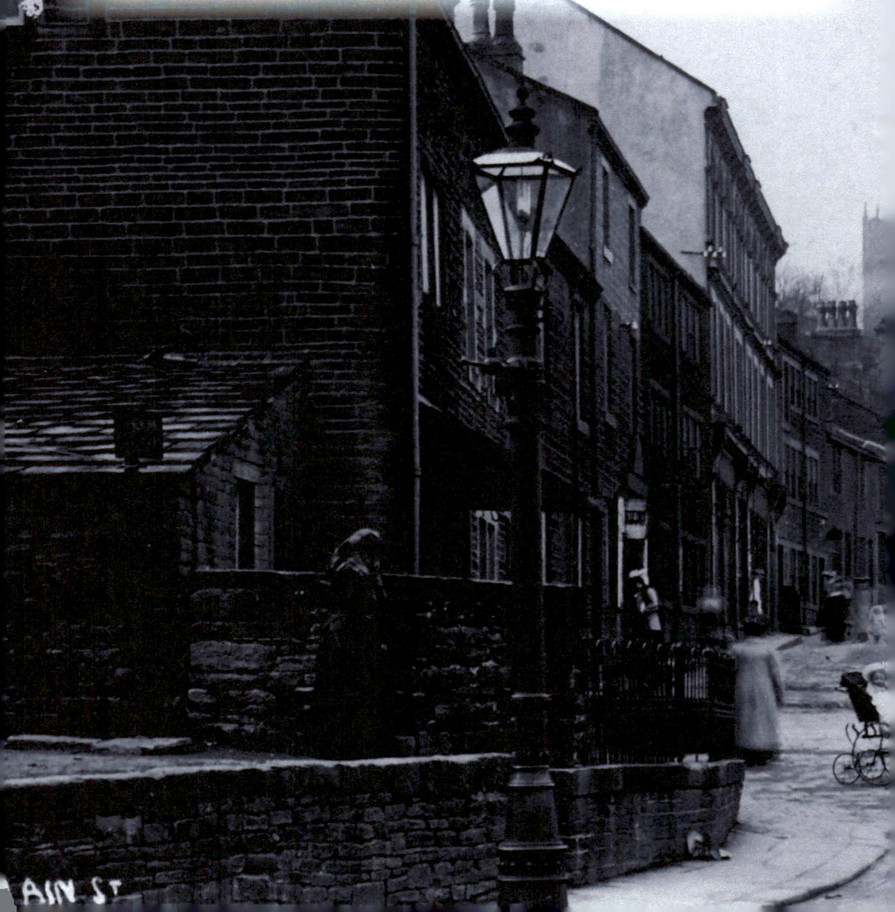

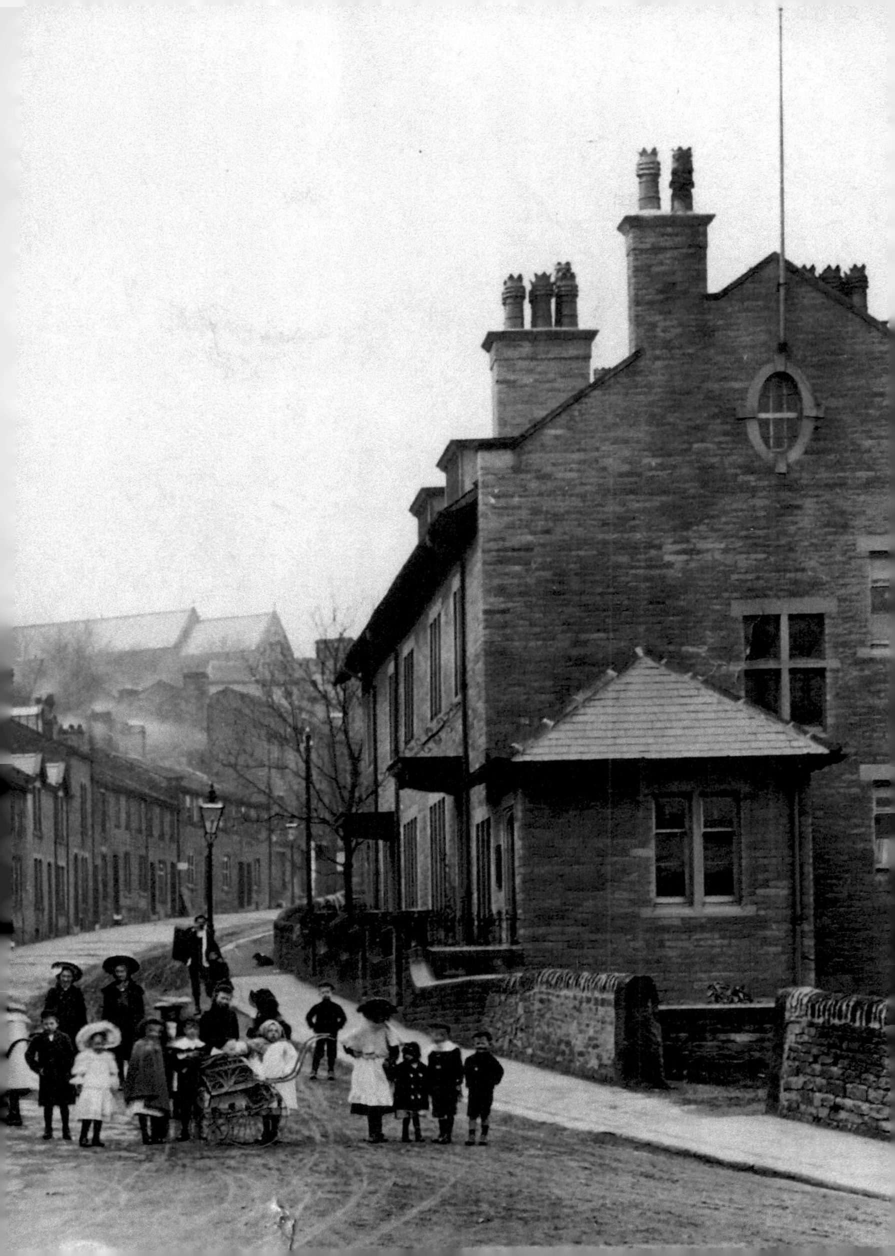

# 20. MAIN STREET

Looking down the street from the Fleece Inn, the predominantly nineteenth-century character of much of Main Street is apparent. Most of these houses date from the first half of the century. The three-storey building immediately above the co-op is perhaps the oldest building in this view. Once home to West Parker's 'Hospital for Umbrellas' and now a restaurant, it is one of the best buildings in Main Street and was built around 1800.

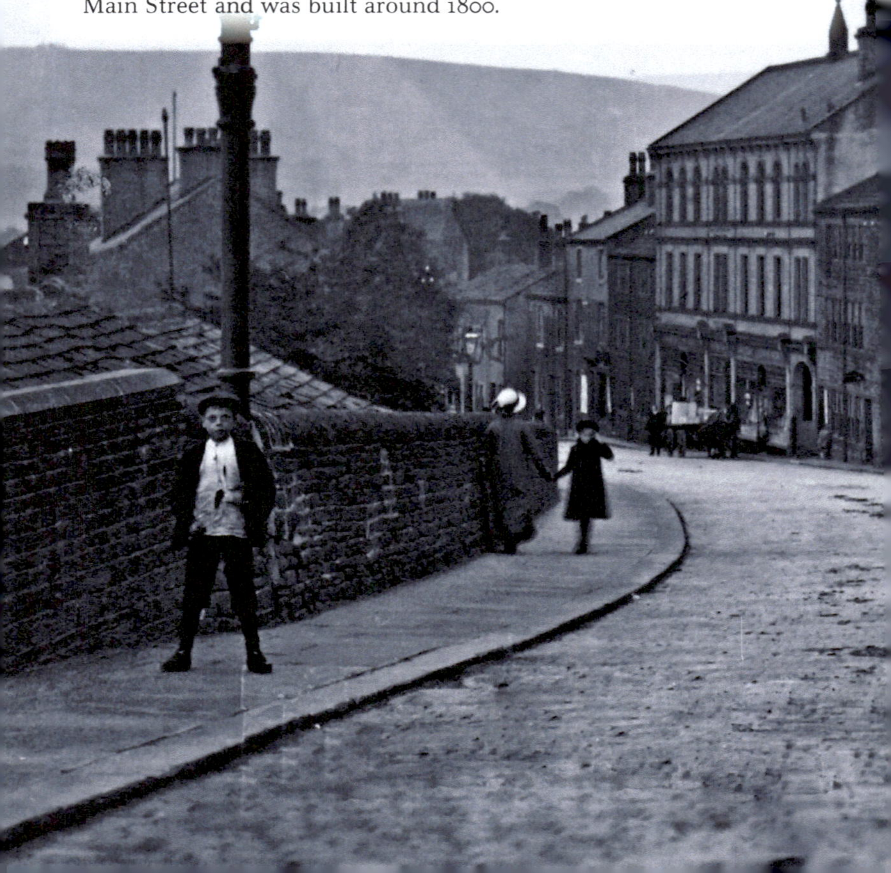

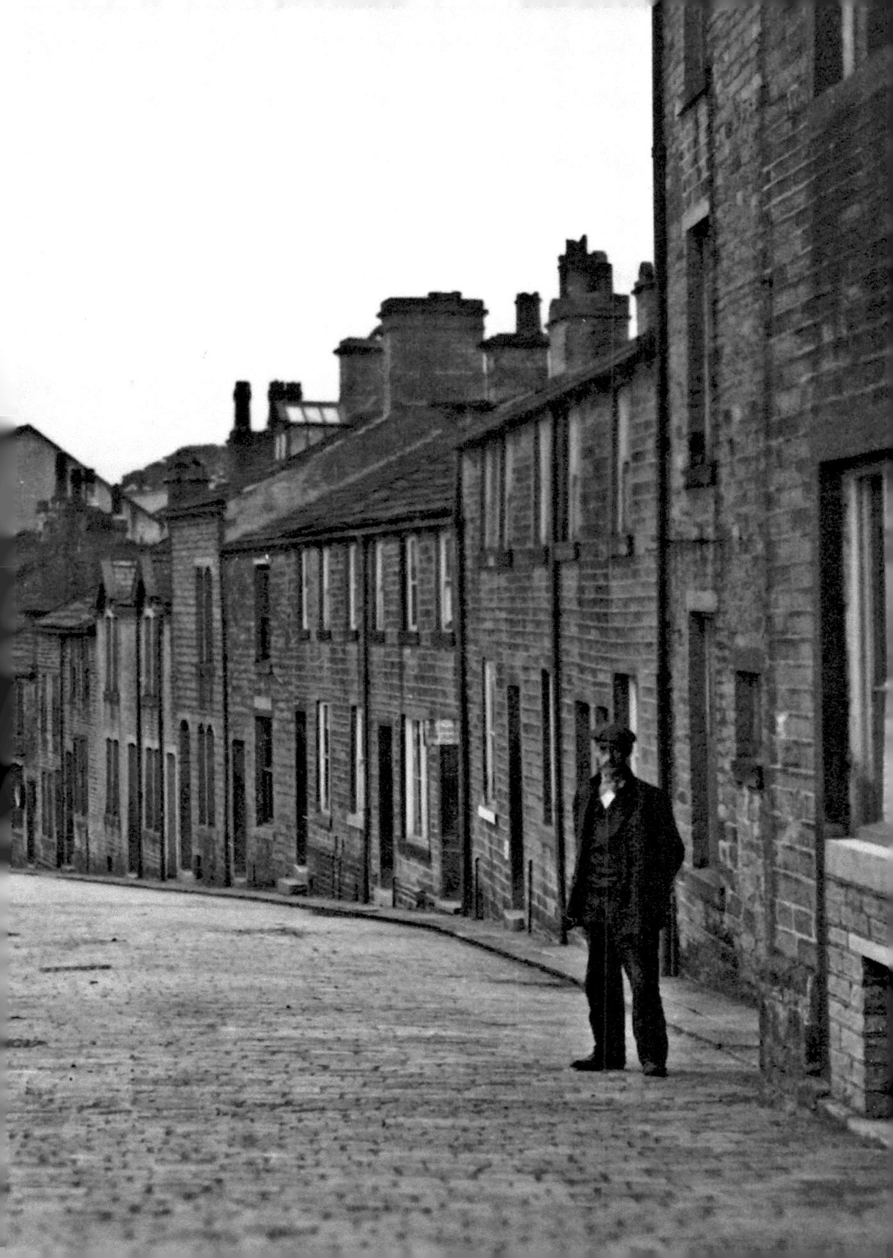

# 21. FLEECE INN

The Fleece appears in the trade directories from 1822 when White's was the first directory to have an entry for Haworth. It has recently been discovered that it opened in 1756 – the year after the road became a turnpike. It was here that the Keighley poet and showman Bill o'th' Hoylus End displayed 'The Great South American War Pig' in 1853.

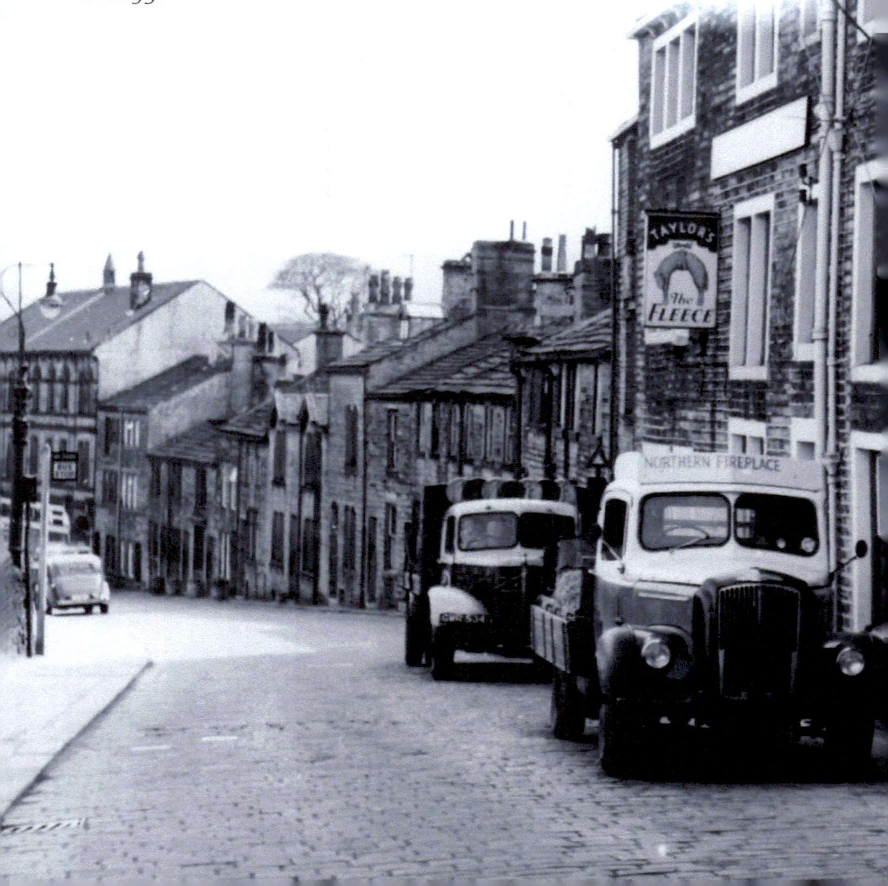

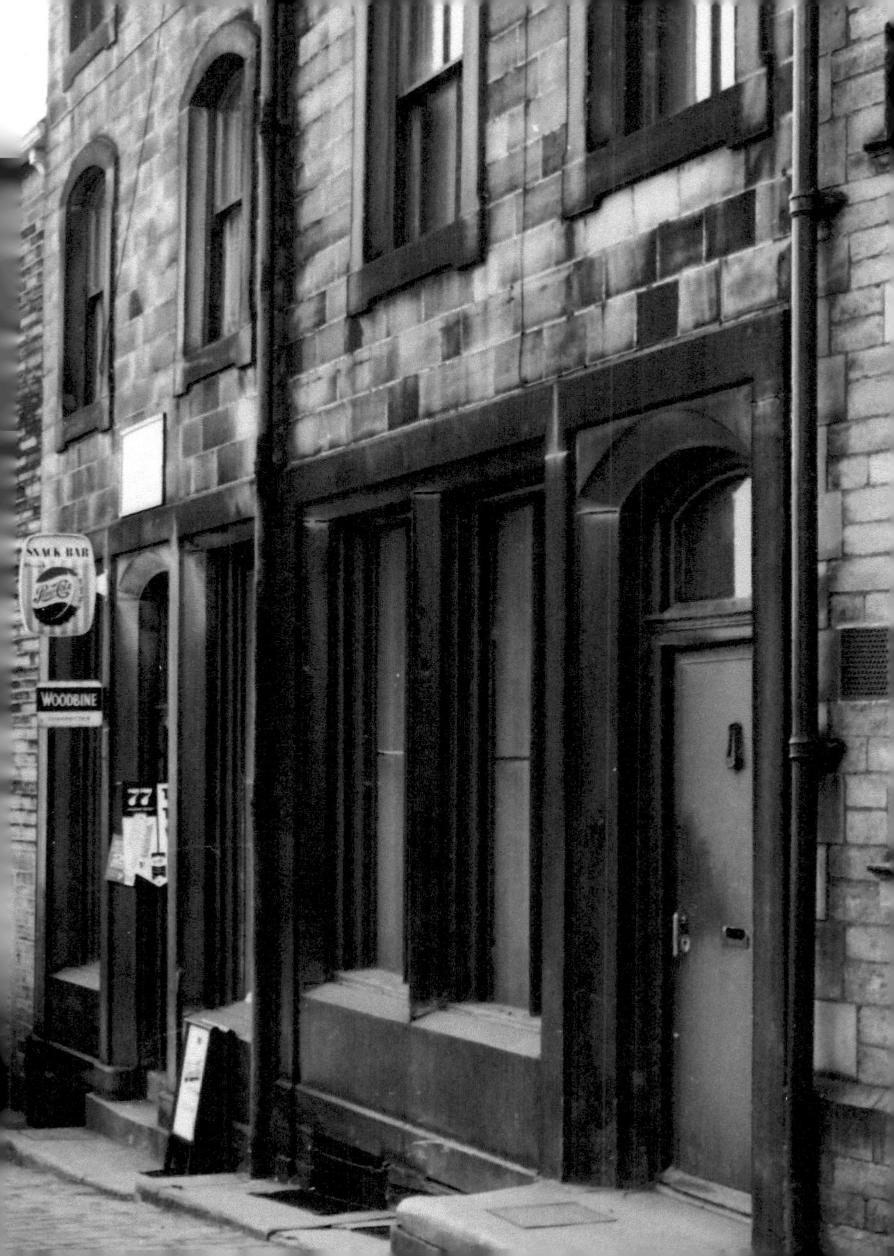

SNACK BAR
Pepsi-Cola
WOODBINE
77

# 22. BUTT LANE

Butt Lane now connects Main Street directly with the railway station, but it used to take a different line. Before the school was built in 1896, Butt Lane turned left across the school grounds to join Acre Lane, which runs down to Mill Hill farm and Lower Mill Hill farm (whose barn occupied what is now the bottom of Butt Lane). The park entrance now follows the oddly shaped field corner.

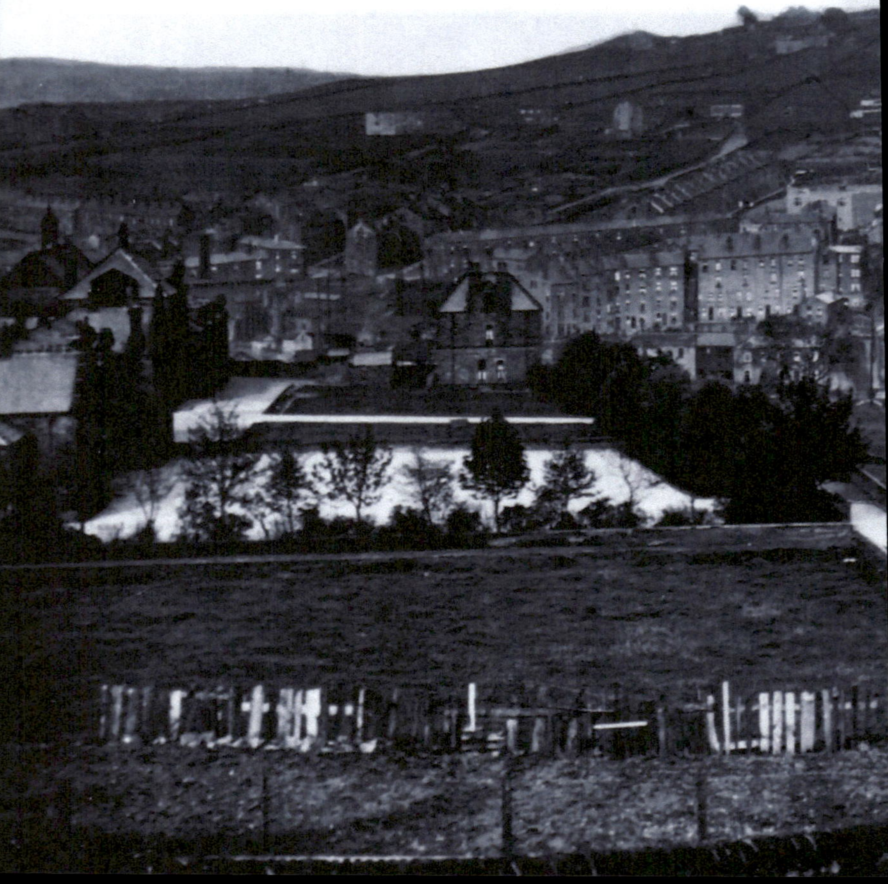

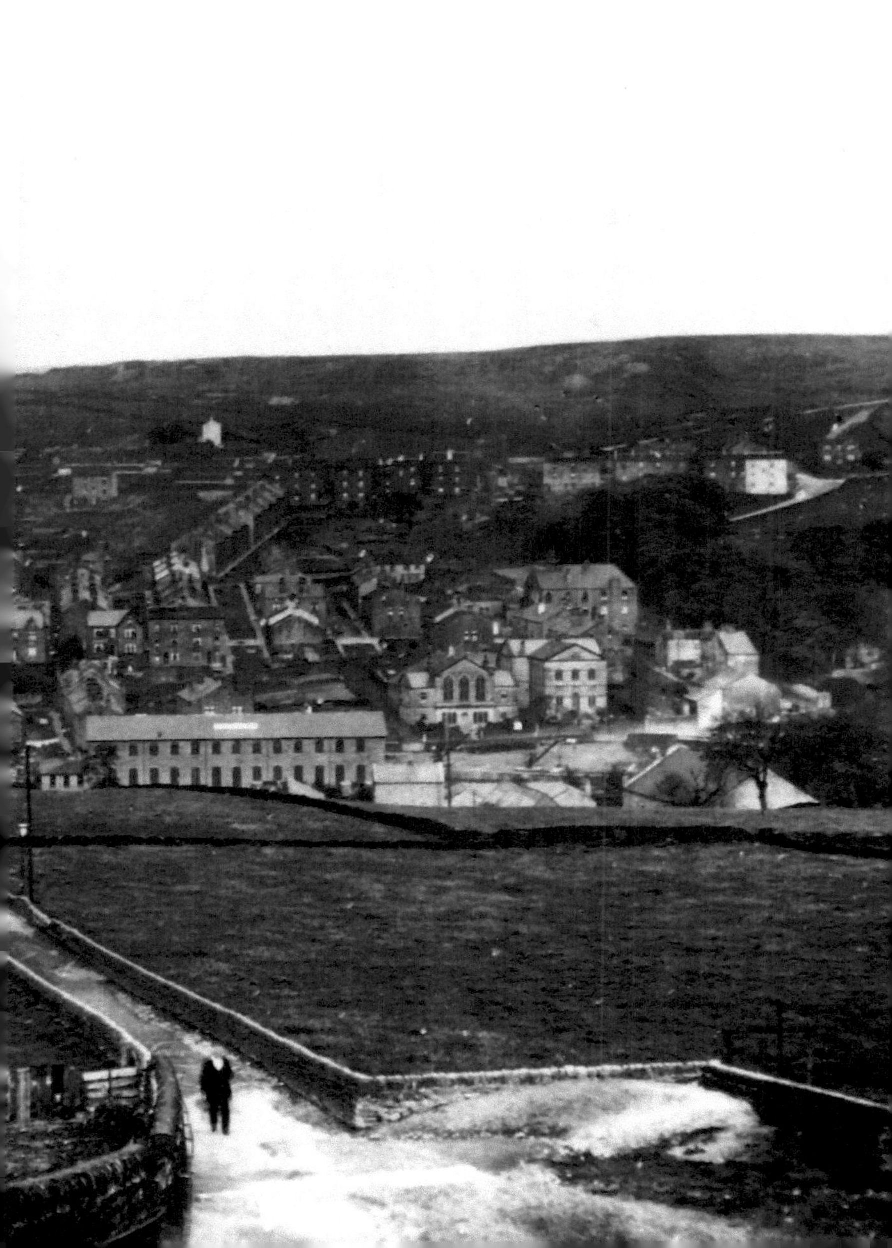

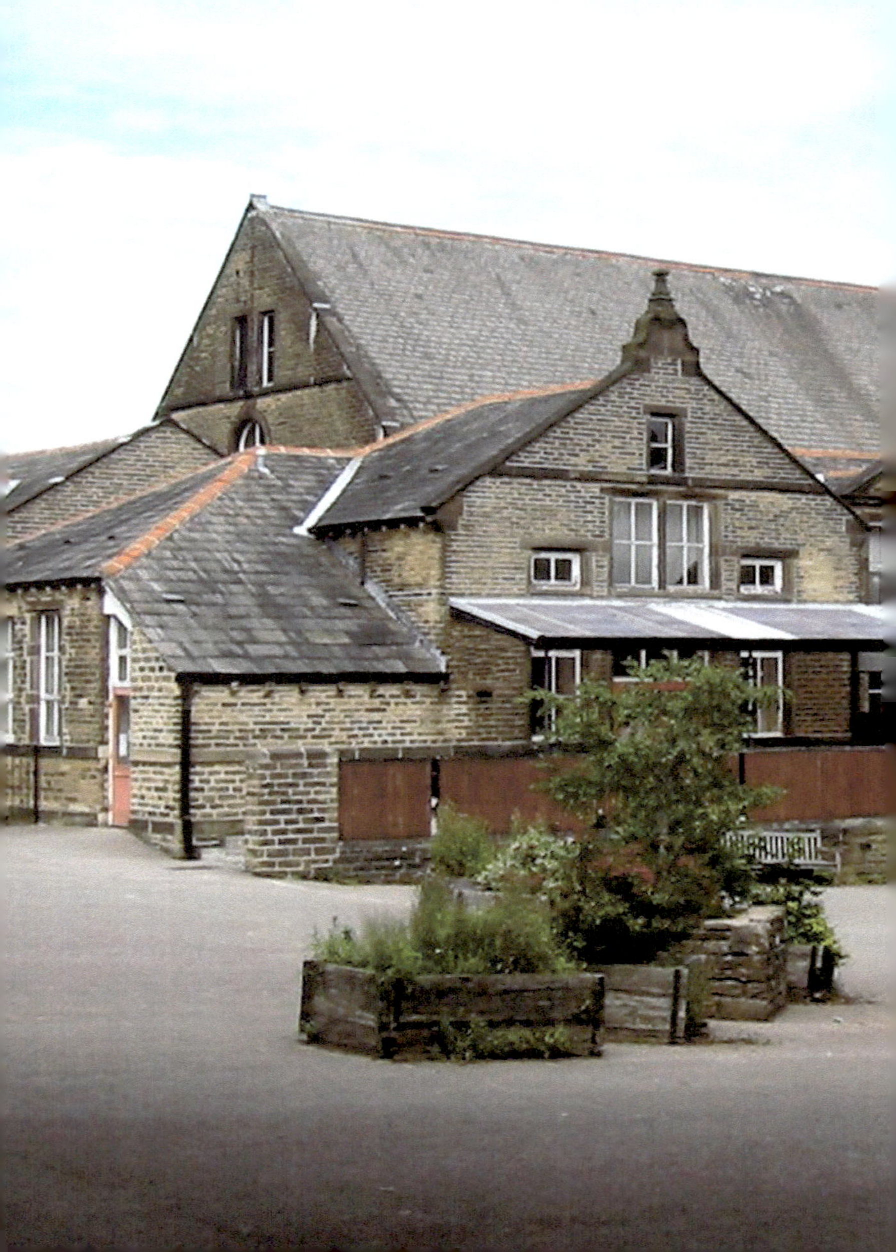

# 23. BUTT LANE SCHOOLS

This fine photograph of the new Butt Lane Schools (*inset*) accompanied a petition by the children to Andrew Carnegie appealing for his help in providing Haworth with a public library. Owing to strife within the Haworth Council this did not happen – in fact, Haworth is still waiting for a library. In the 100 years between the two photographs little had changed; however, the main school building has since been converted into housing.

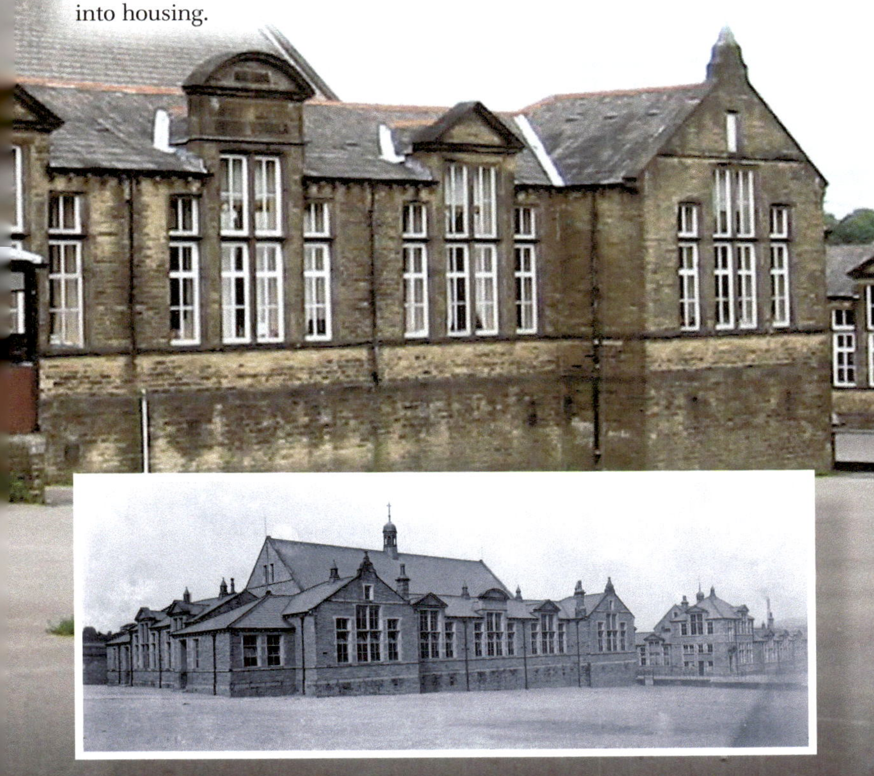

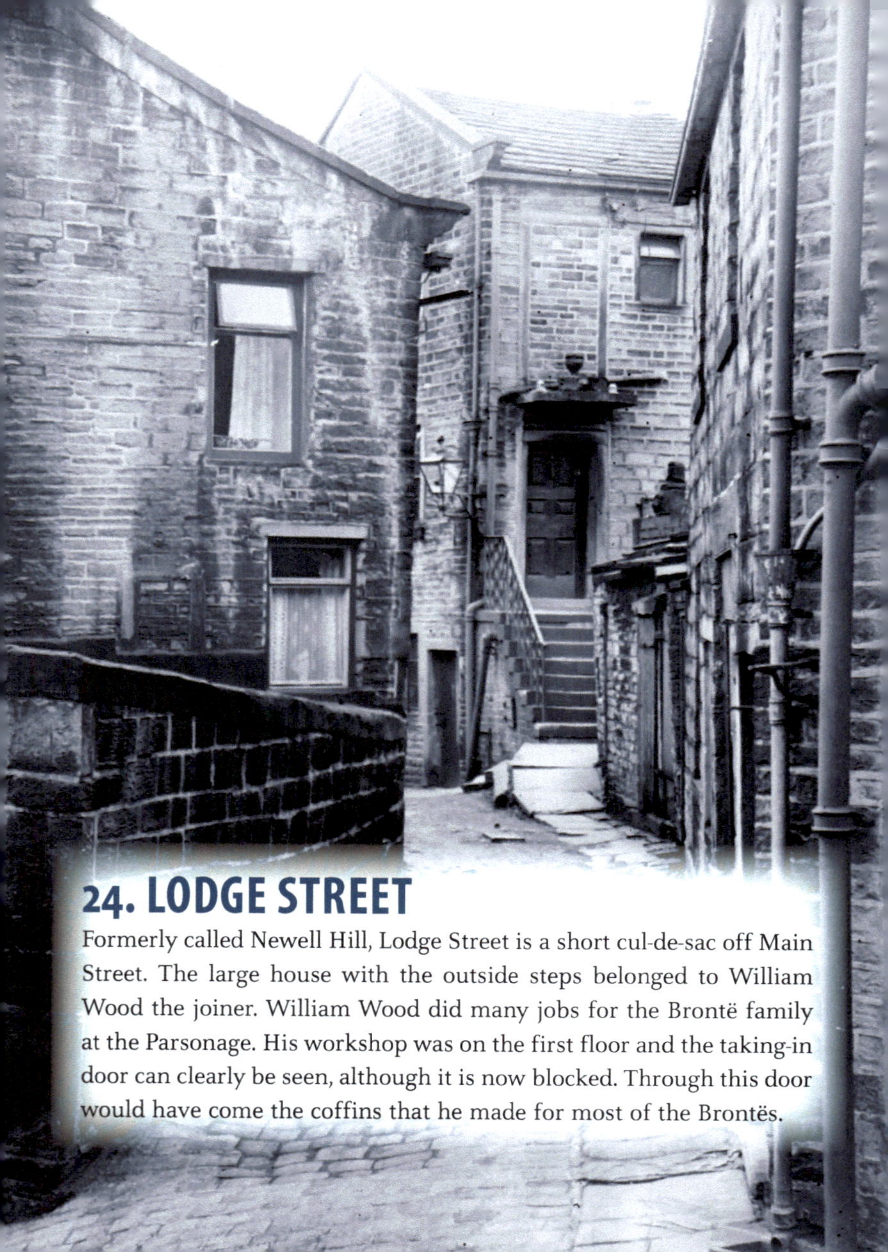

# 24. LODGE STREET

Formerly called Newell Hill, Lodge Street is a short cul-de-sac off Main Street. The large house with the outside steps belonged to William Wood the joiner. William Wood did many jobs for the Brontë family at the Parsonage. His workshop was on the first floor and the taking-in door can clearly be seen, although it is now blocked. Through this door would have come the coffins that he made for most of the Brontës.

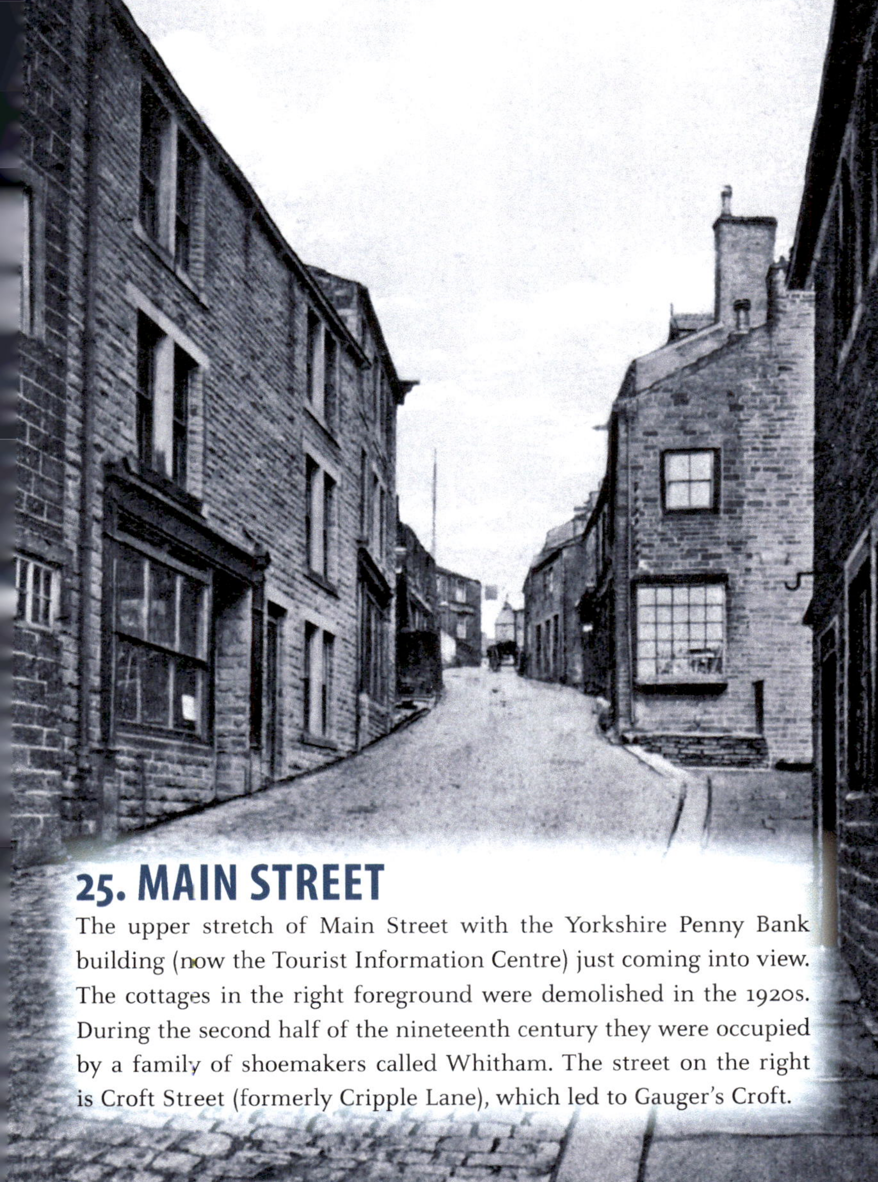

# 25. MAIN STREET

The upper stretch of Main Street with the Yorkshire Penny Bank building (now the Tourist Information Centre) just coming into view. The cottages in the right foreground were demolished in the 1920s. During the second half of the nineteenth century they were occupied by a family of shoemakers called Whitham. The street on the right is Croft Street (formerly Cripple Lane), which led to Gauger's Croft.

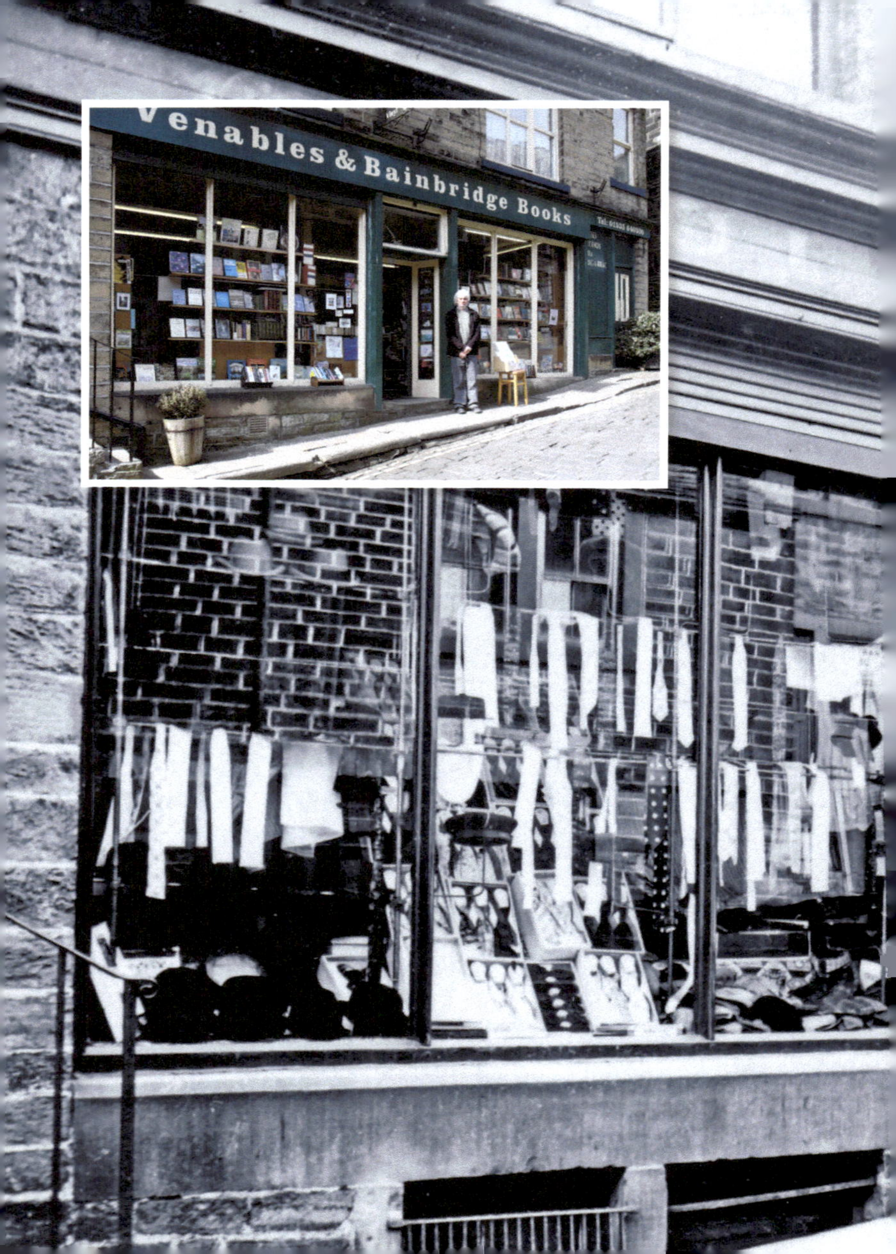

Venables & Bainbridge Books
Tel: 01535 646000

# 26. MAIN STREET

Manasseh Hollindrake exemplifies Victorian Haworth's fondness for resounding Old Testament names. He ran this draper's shop at No. 111 Main Street from around 1860 to 1897. He was also a farmer from the 1880s, no doubt in connection with his son James's butcher's shop at No. 66 Main Street. He died in 1919 at the age of eighty-two. The figure at the shop door (in the older photograph) may be his wife, Mary, who died in 1897.

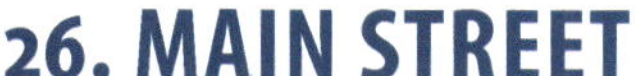

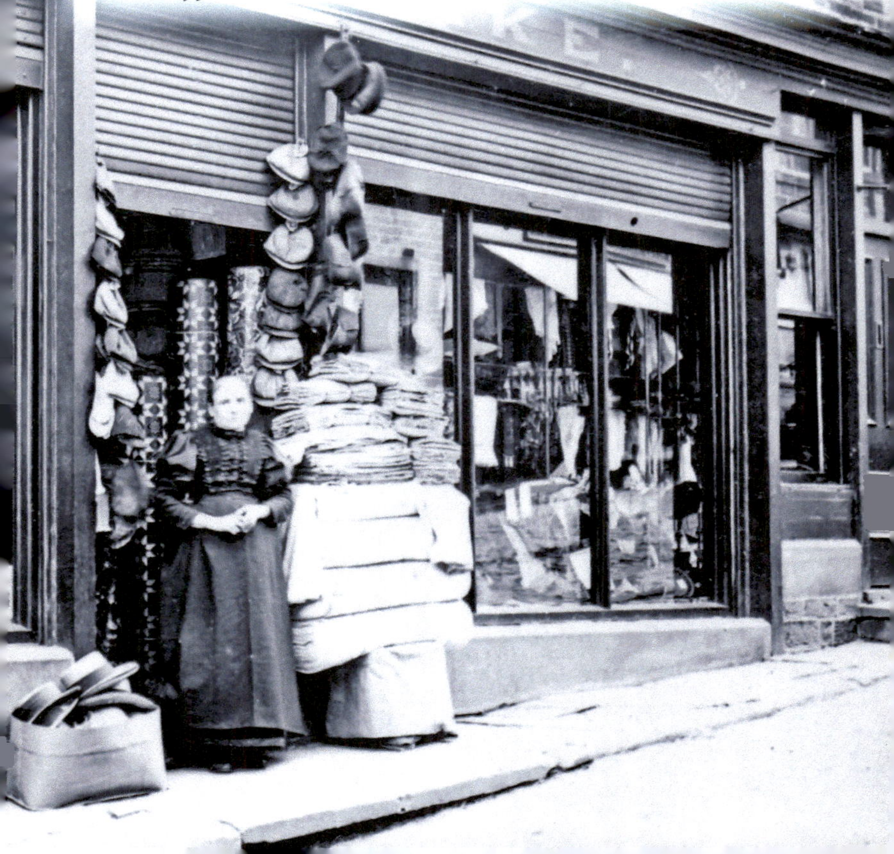

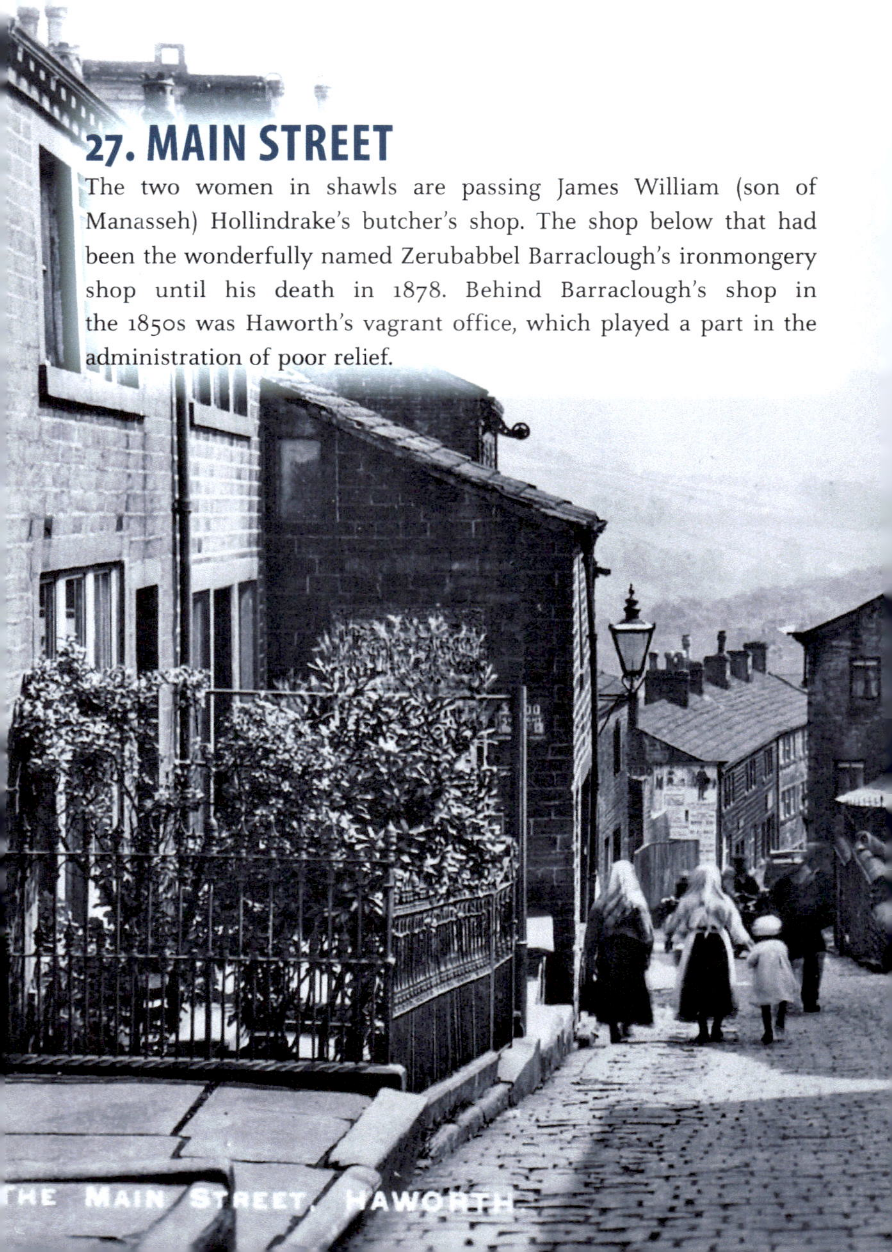

# 27. MAIN STREET

The two women in shawls are passing James William (son of Manasseh) Hollindrake's butcher's shop. The shop below that had been the wonderfully named Zerubabbel Barraclough's ironmongery shop until his death in 1878. Behind Barraclough's shop in the 1850s was Haworth's vagrant office, which played a part in the administration of poor relief.

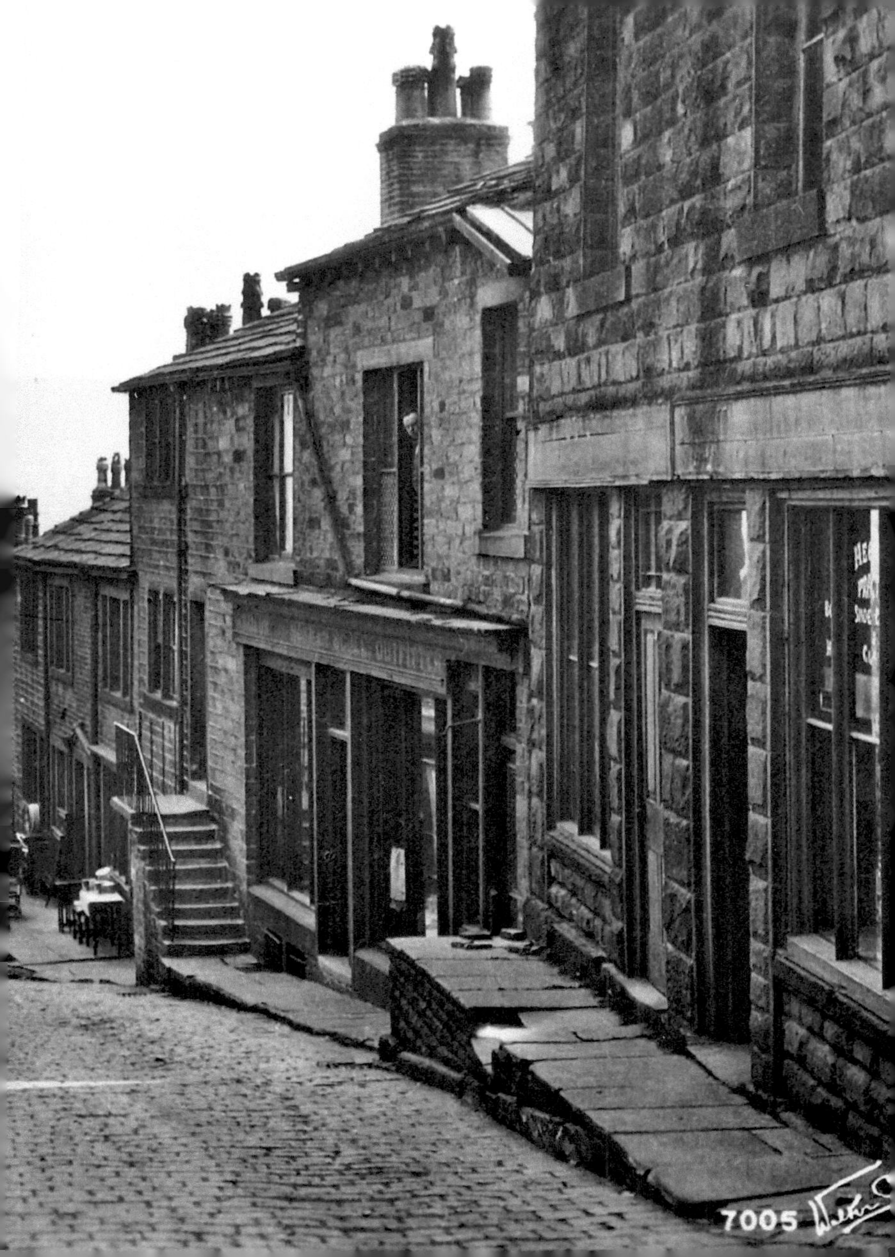
7005

# 28. MAIN STREET

Looking across Main Street from the Black Bull car park we can see the archway that led through to the area of housing called Old Piccadilly. This was also known as Brandy Row and Gauger's Croft. The building through which the archway passes belonged to Richard Roberts Thomas in 1850. His trade as a wine and spirit merchant lies behind the names Brandy Row and Gauger's Croft (a gauger being an excise man).

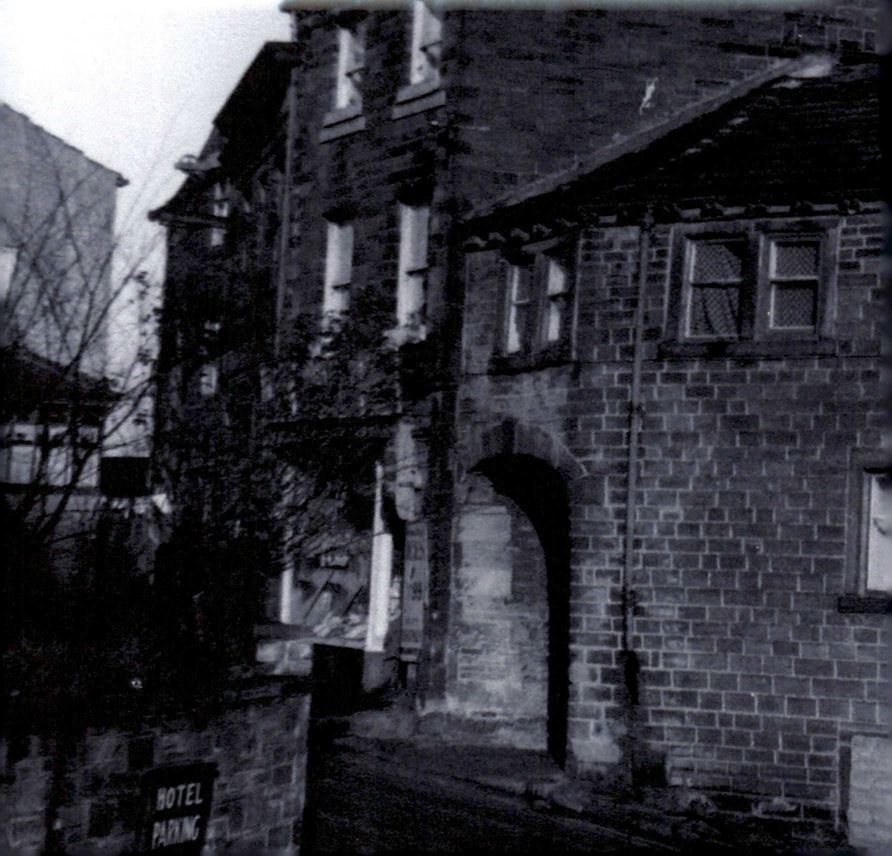

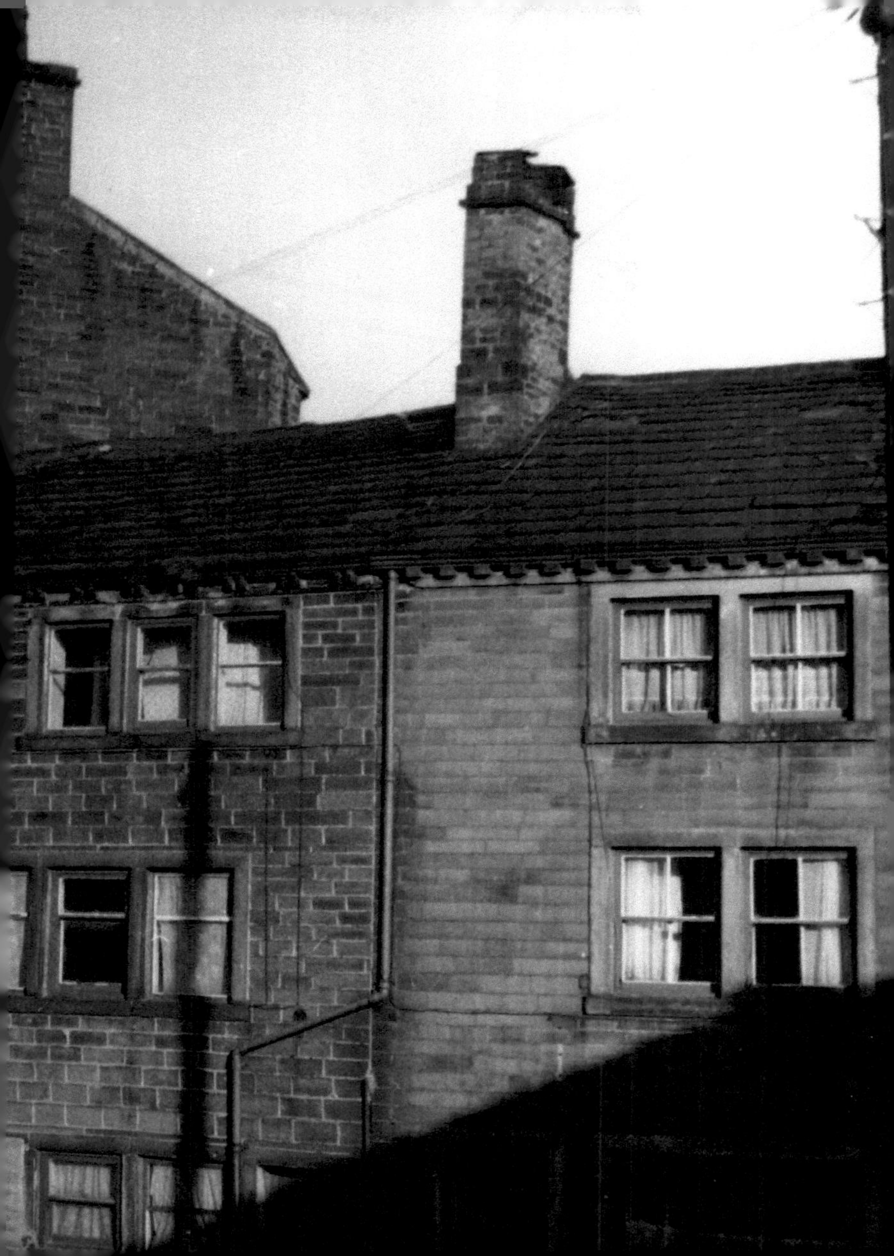

# 29. MAIN STREET

The Liberal Club was built in 1853 as the Black Bull lecture rooms. At first it was the home of the Haworth Mechanics' Institute, which moved here from Lodge Street. They left in 1877 but were to return in 1894. In 1881, the building reopened as the Haworth Liberal Club. The Liberal Club closed in the 1960s, since when it has housed a variety of shops.

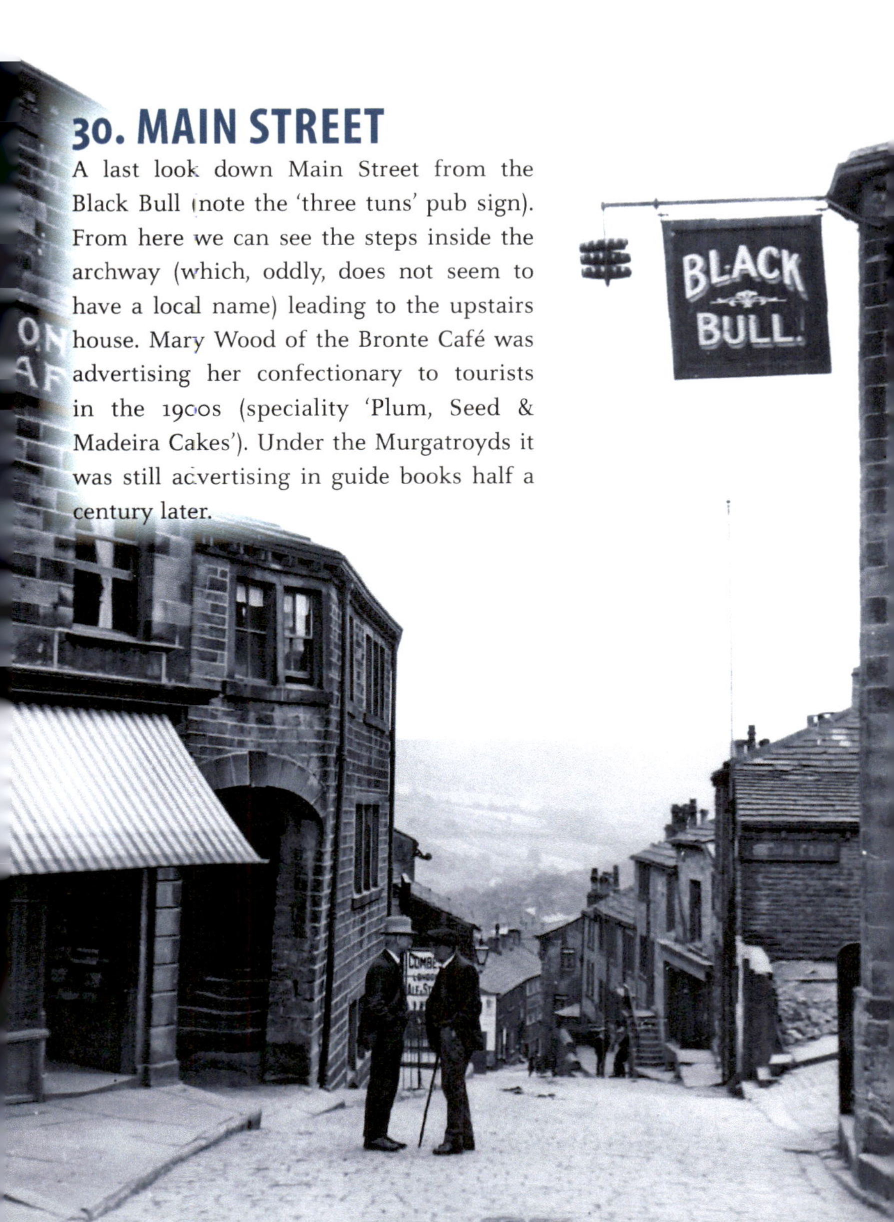


# 30. MAIN STREET

A last look down Main Street from the Black Bull (note the 'three tuns' pub sign). From here we can see the steps inside the archway (which, oddly, does not seem to have a local name) leading to the upstairs house. Mary Wood of the Bronte Café was advertising her confectionary to tourists in the 1900s (speciality 'Plum, Seed & Madeira Cakes'). Under the Murgatroyds it was still advertising in guide books half a century later.

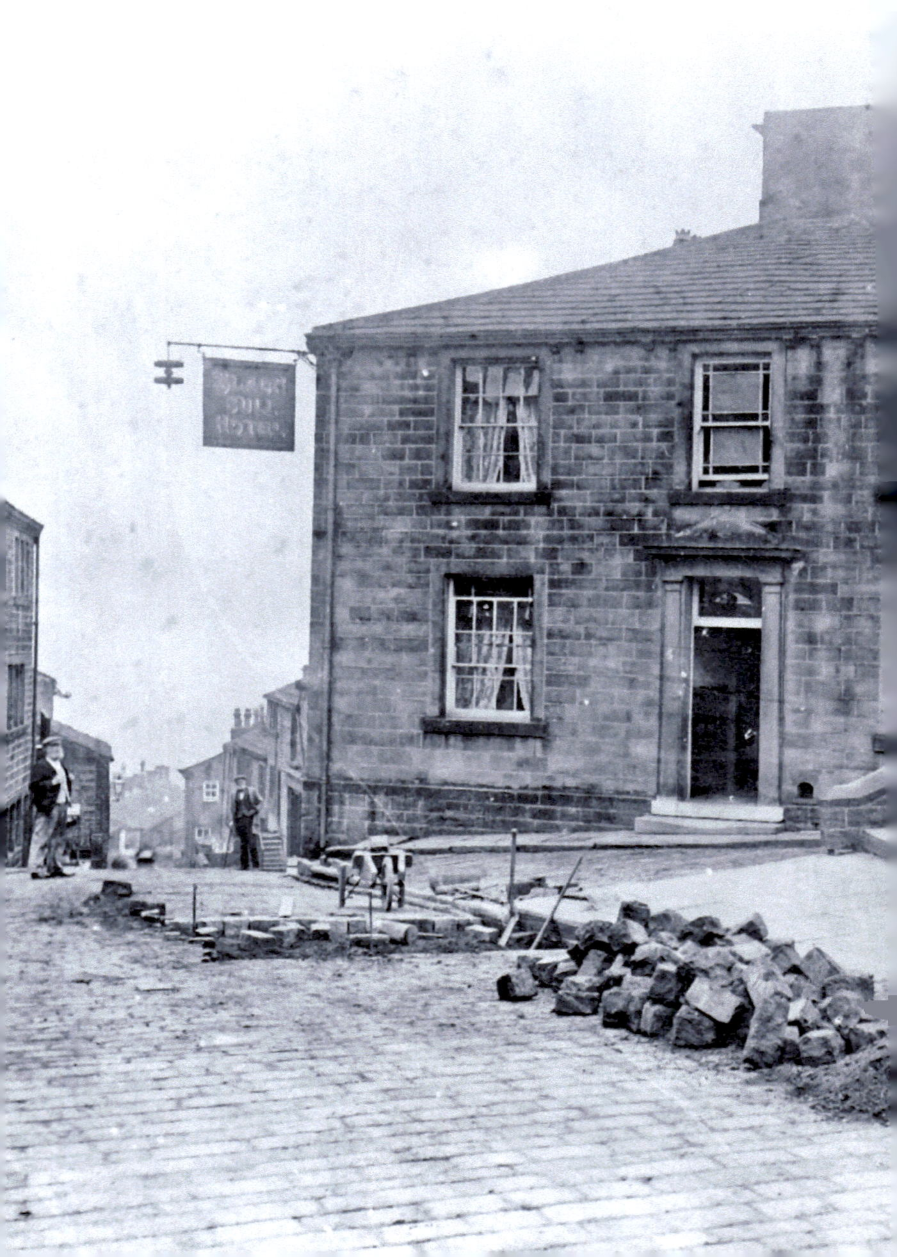
BLACK BULL
BULL
HOTEL

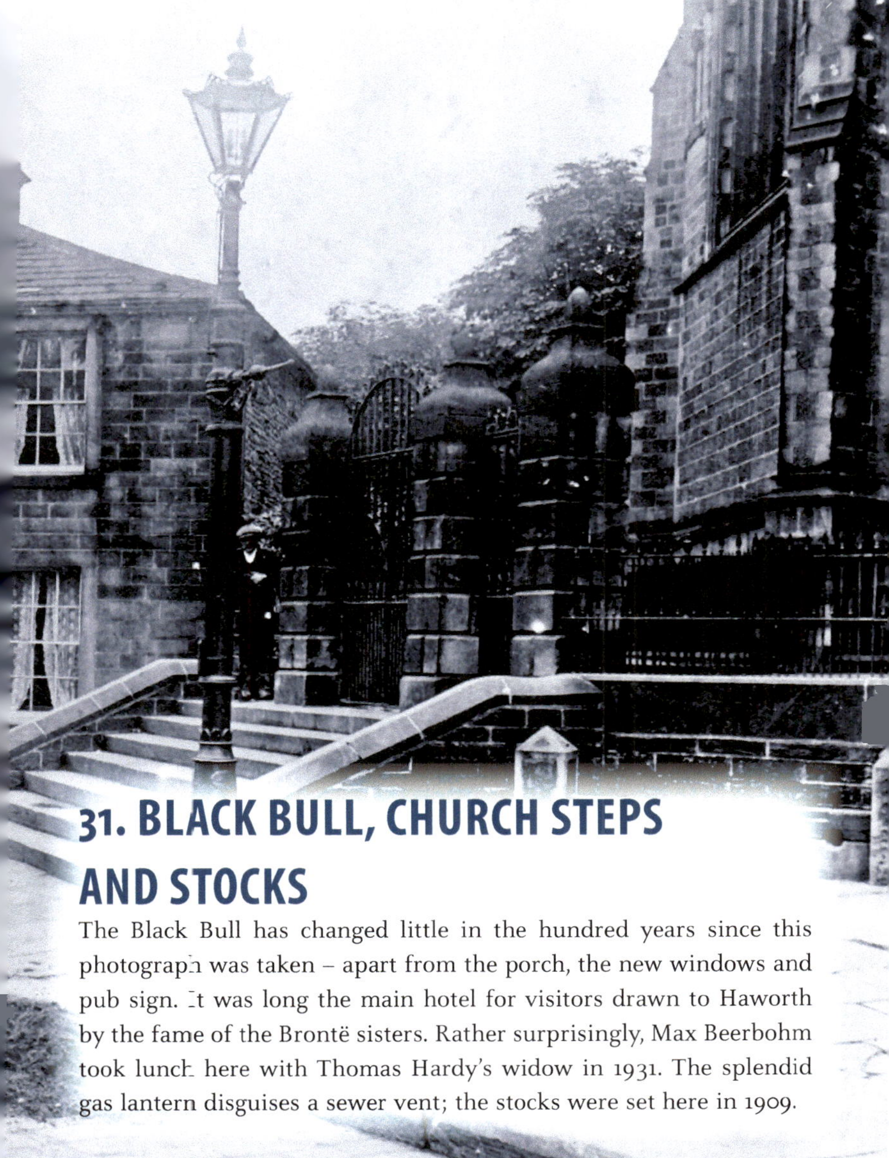

# 31. BLACK BULL, CHURCH STEPS AND STOCKS

The Black Bull has changed little in the hundred years since this photograph was taken – apart from the porch, the new windows and pub sign. It was long the main hotel for visitors drawn to Haworth by the fame of the Brontë sisters. Rather surprisingly, Max Beerbohm took lunch here with Thomas Hardy's widow in 1931. The splendid gas lantern disguises a sewer vent; the stocks were set here in 1909.

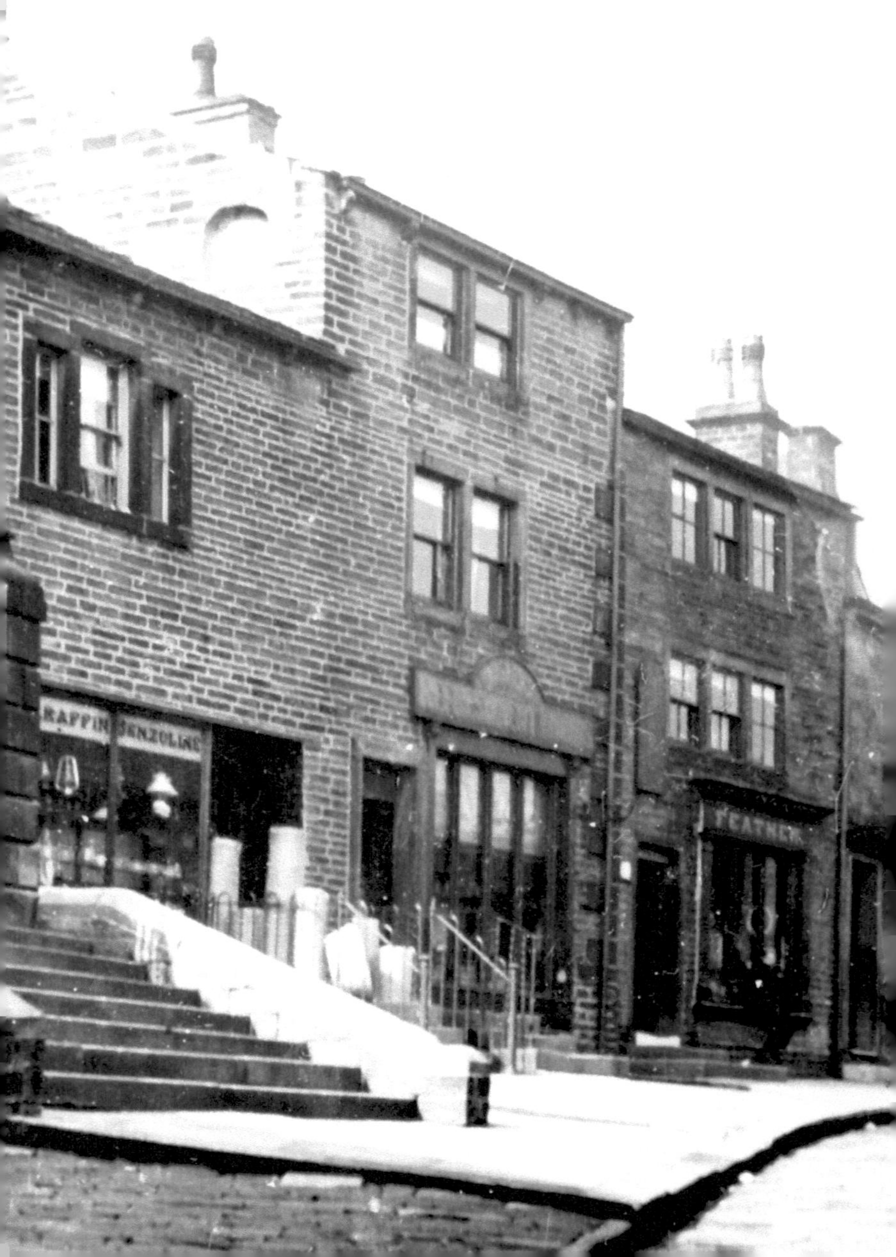
RAPPIN  BENZOLINE
FEATHER

# 32. MAIN STREET

This photograph can be dated to 1893/94 by Anne Lee's name on the White Lion. Right of the Lion is the bow-windowed frontage of the Mechanics' Institute. The Mechanics moved here from the Liberal Club in 1877; in 1894, the Yorkshire Penny Bank bought the building from them and converted it to what we see today. The Mechanics moved back to the Liberal Club and stayed there until 1925 when they closed.

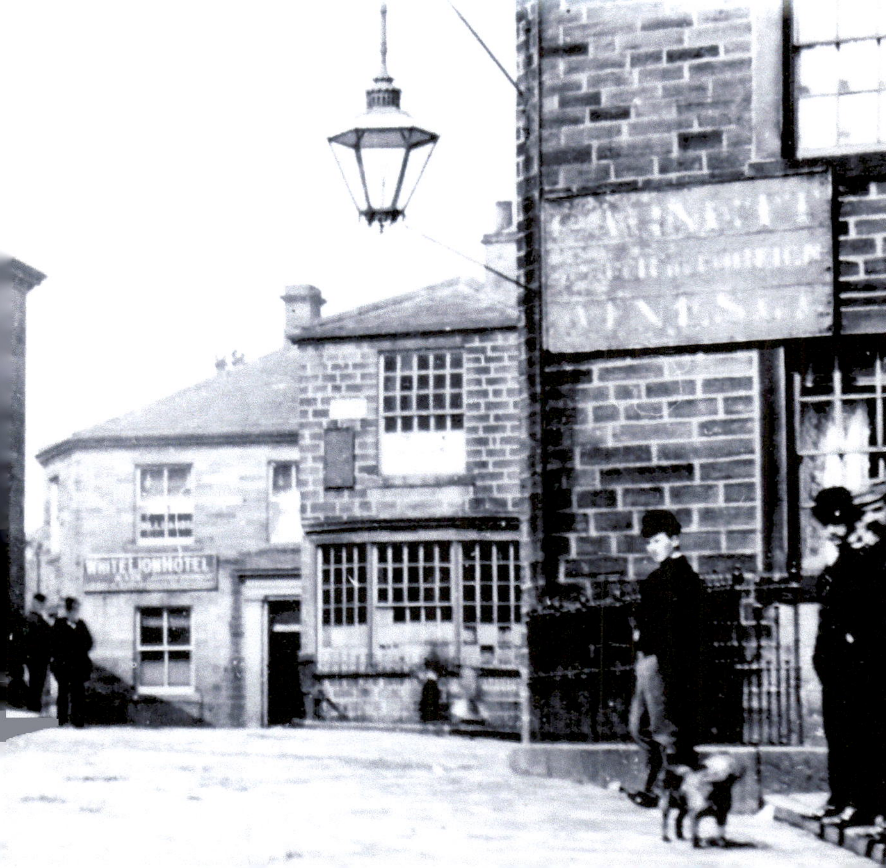

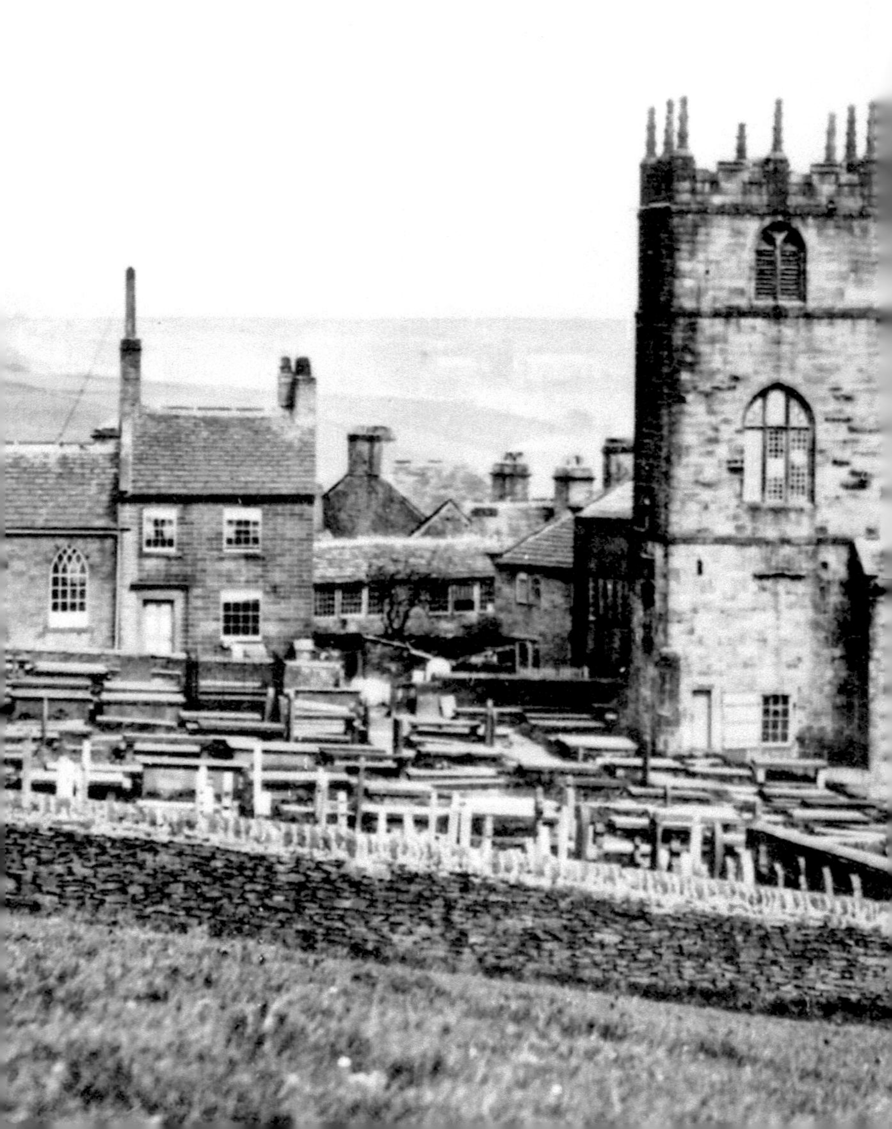

# 33. OLD CHURCH

On the far left is part of the Sunday school, which was built by Patrick Brontë in 1832 and extended in 1851. On the right-hand side of the Sunday school is Sexton House, built by John Brown in 1838. The gravestones nearest to the camera are quite new – this section of the graveyard was opened in 1856. The tower is ancient but the rest of the old church was built in 1755; the new church opened in 1881.

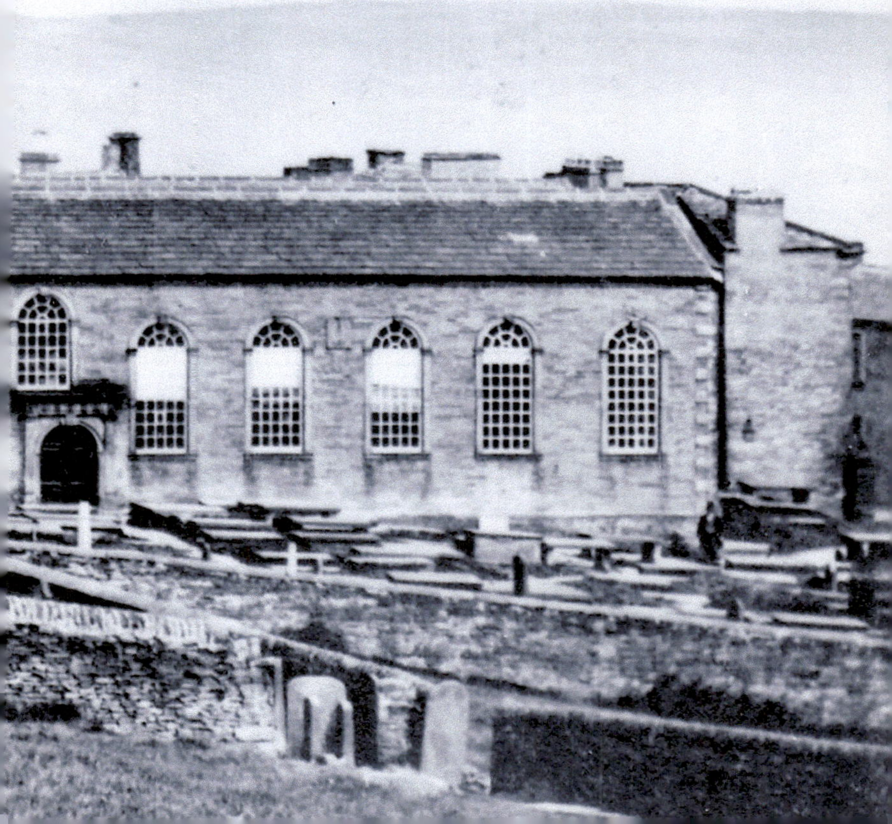

# 34. KING'S ARMS

The King's Arms is a handsome building of the mid-eighteenth century, although a small part of the building near the Fold belongs to the seventeenth century. It was used from 1763 (or possibly a little earlier) as the meeting place for the manorial court. From 1768 it is referred to in the manor court rolls as the 'Manor House of Haworth'. It is last mentioned in this connection in 1870.

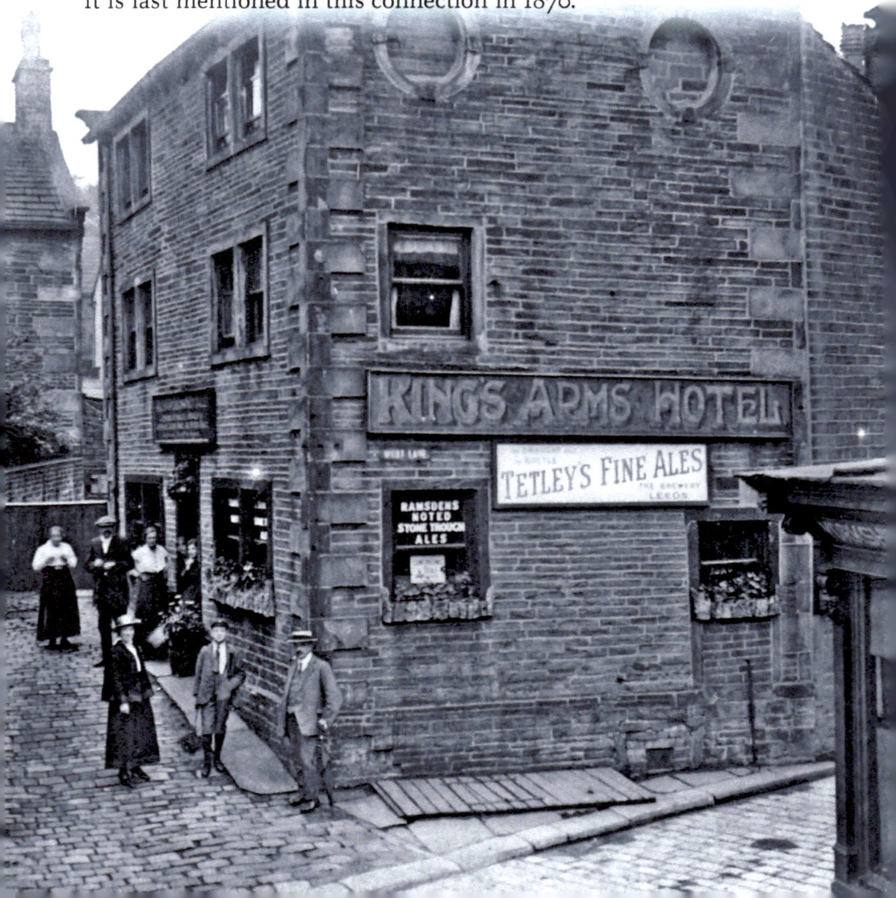

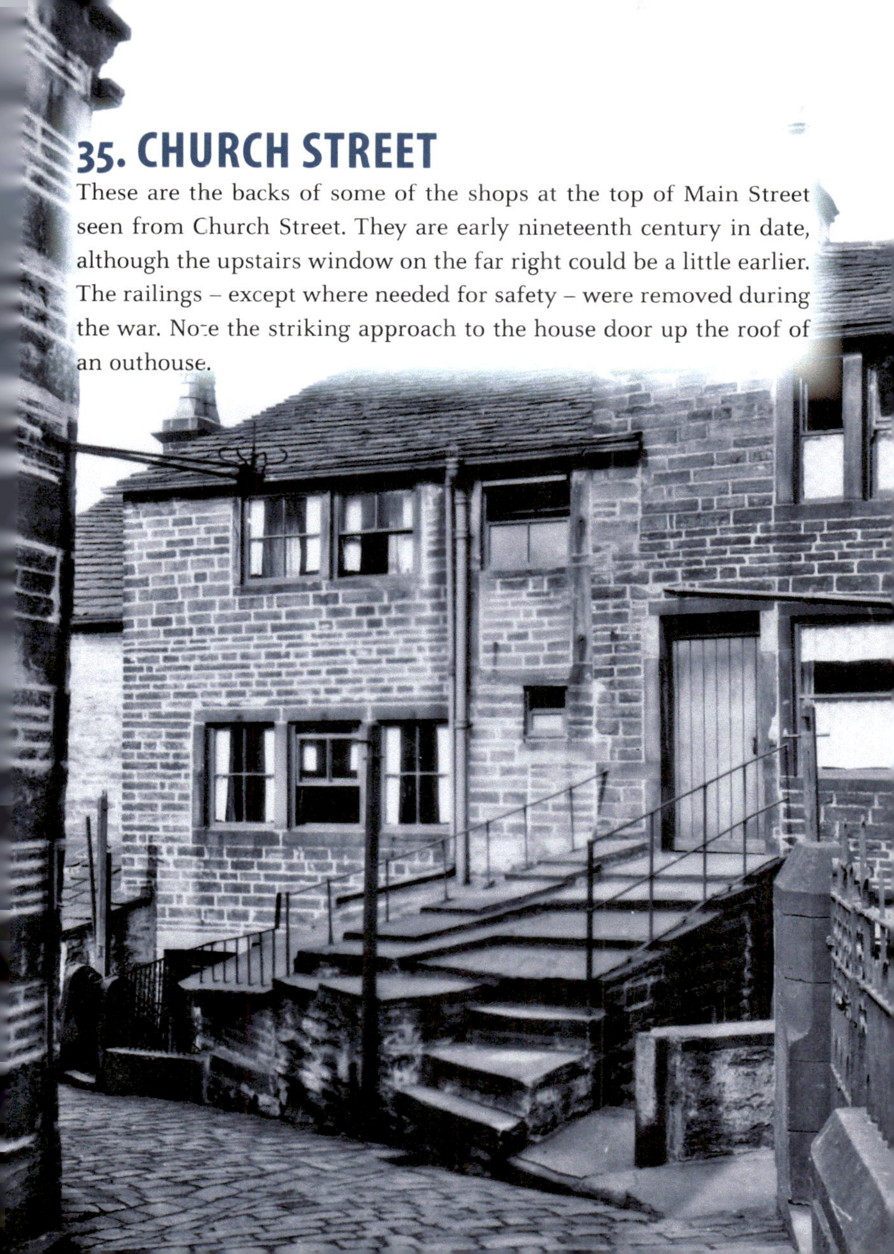

# 35. CHURCH STREET

These are the backs of some of the shops at the top of Main Street seen from Church Street. They are early nineteenth century in date, although the upstairs window on the far right could be a little earlier. The railings – except where needed for safety – were removed during the war. Note the striking approach to the house door up the roof of an outhouse.

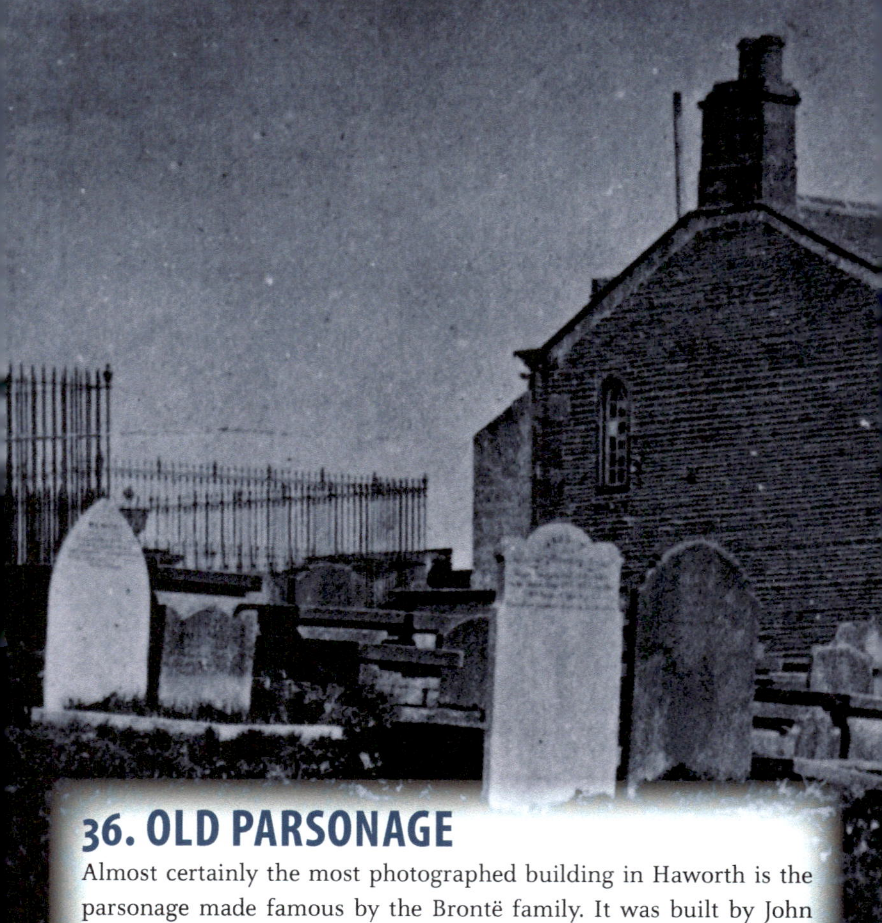

# 36. OLD PARSONAGE

Almost certainly the most photographed building in Haworth is the parsonage made famous by the Brontë family. It was built by John Richardson in 1779 as a more convenient home for the minister than Grimshaw's Sowdens Farm. Brontë came here in 1820 and stayed until his death in 1861. Brontë's successor John Wade added the new wing on the right in 1878. The parsonage became the home of the Brontë Society's museum in 1928.

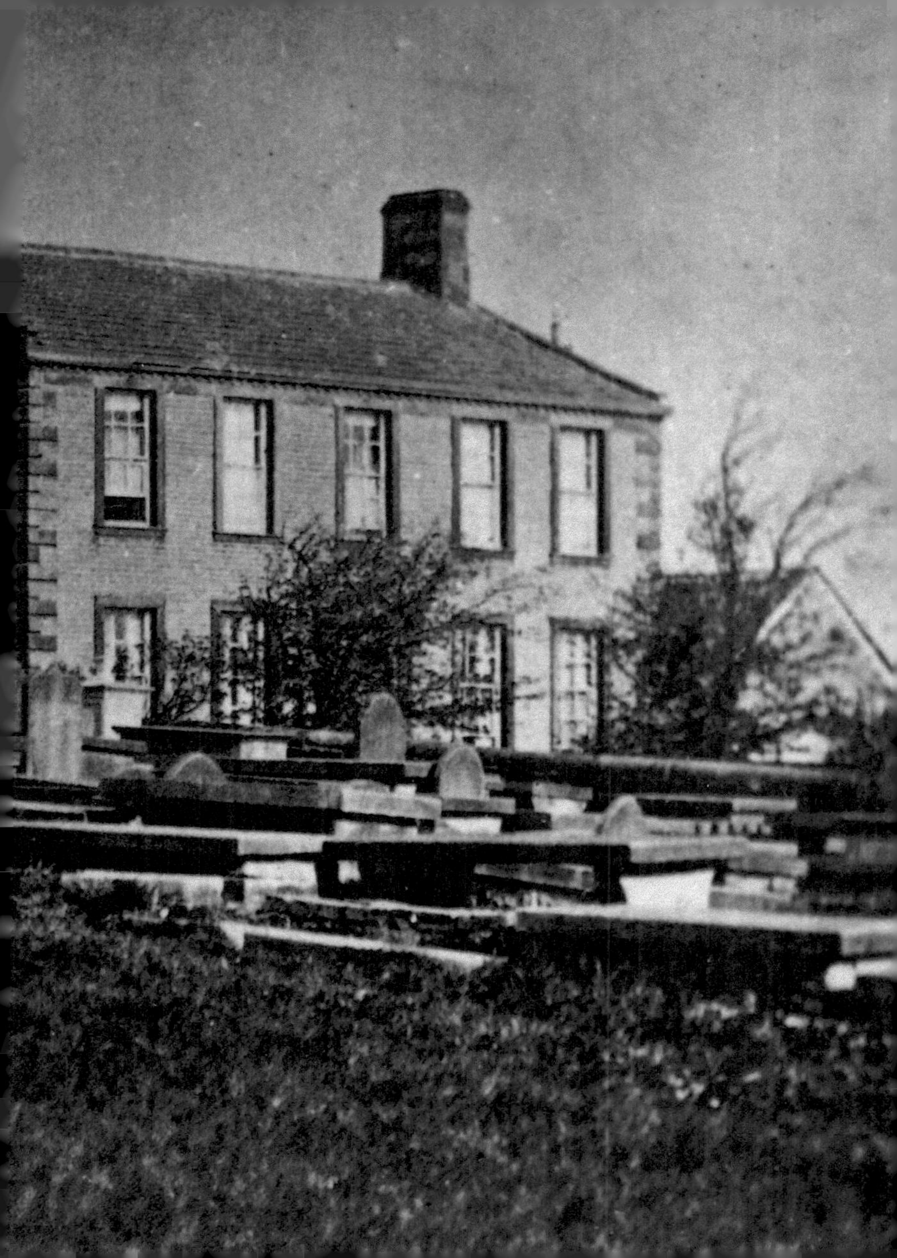

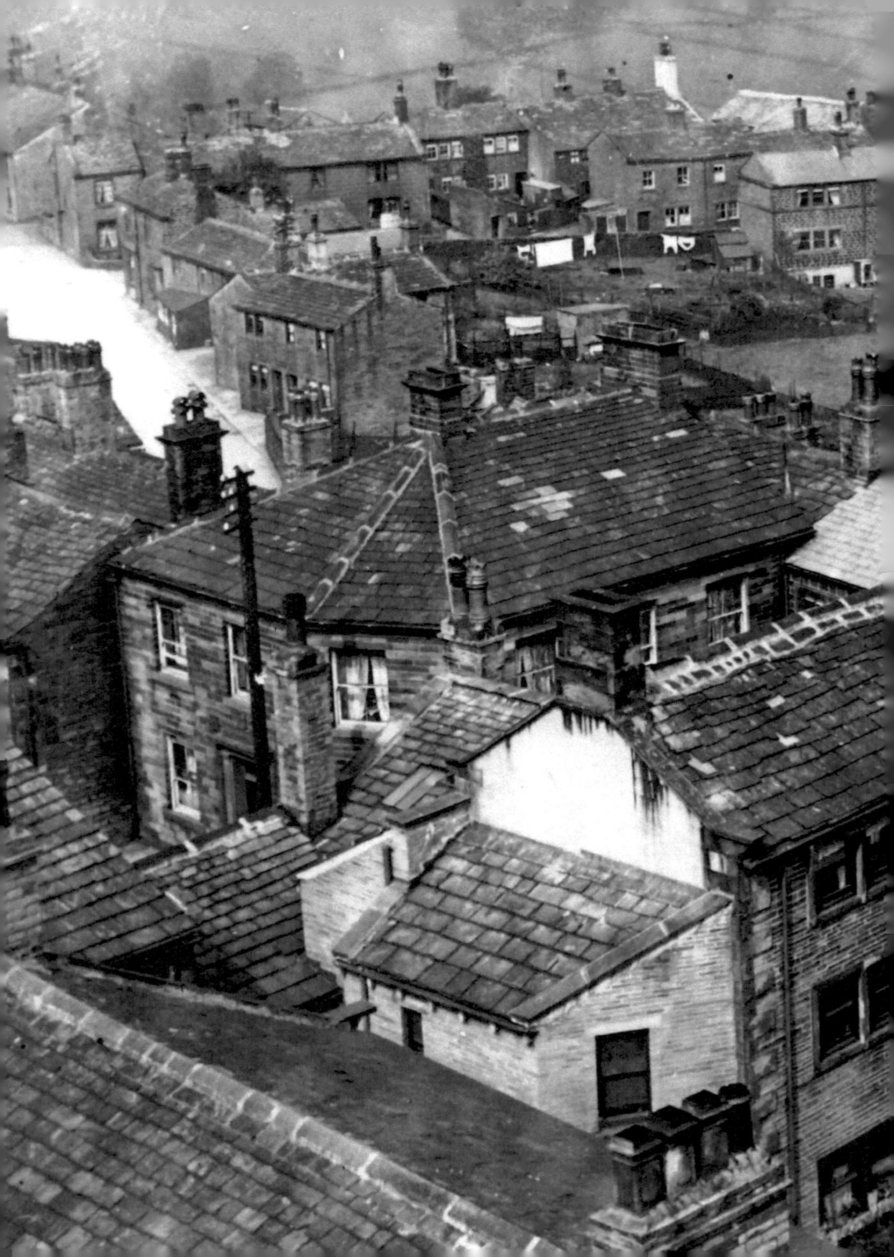

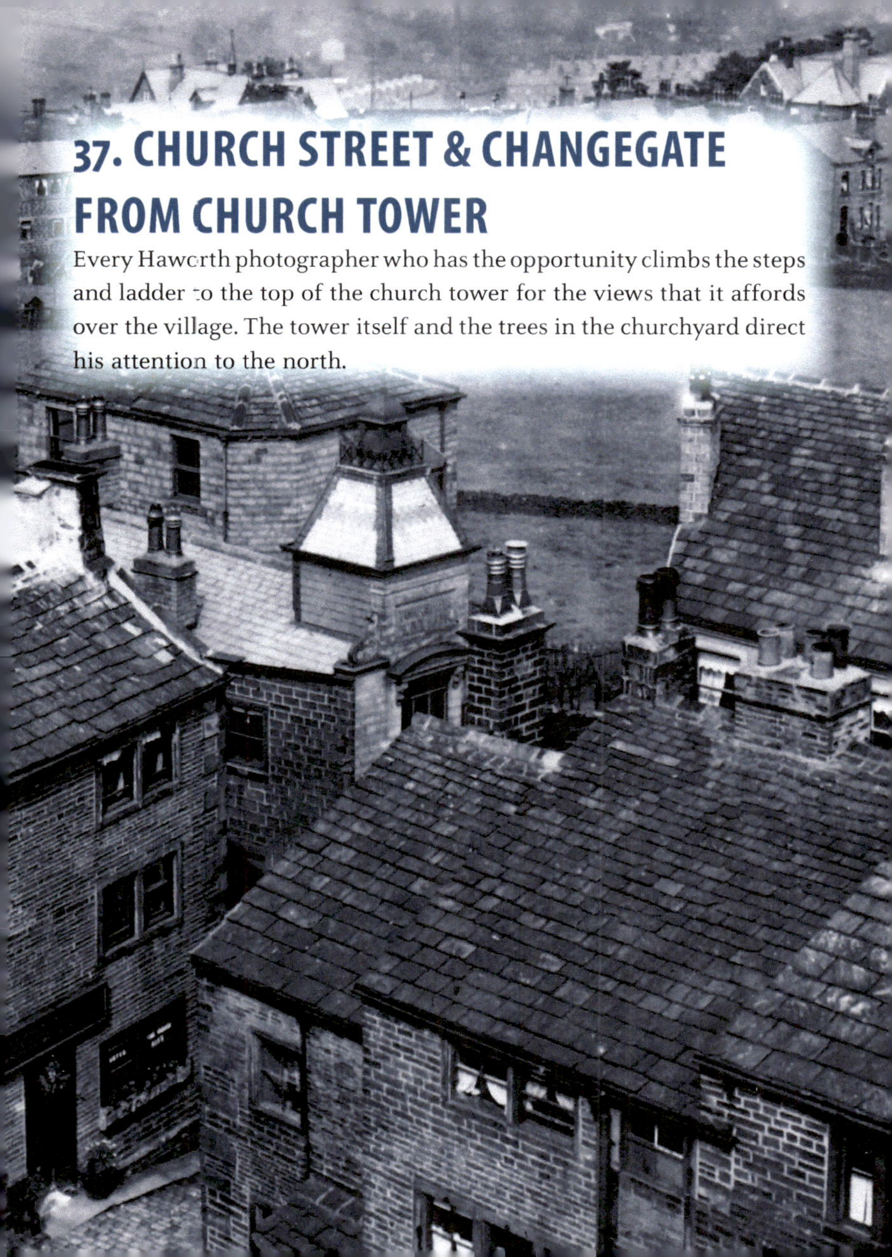

# 37. CHURCH STREET & CHANGEGATE FROM CHURCH TOWER

Every Haworth photographer who has the opportunity climbs the steps and ladder to the top of the church tower for the views that it affords over the village. The tower itself and the trees in the churchyard direct his attention to the north.

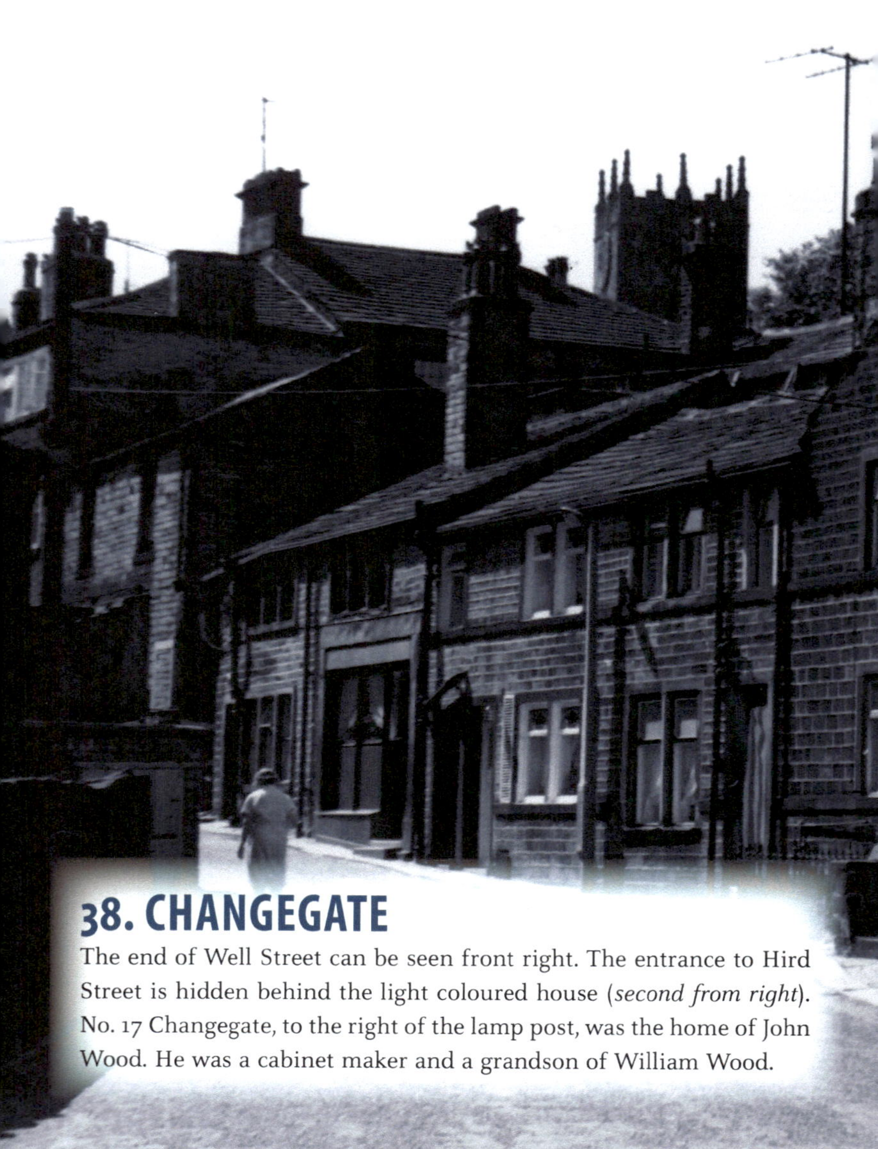

# 38. CHANGEGATE

The end of Well Street can be seen front right. The entrance to Hird Street is hidden behind the light coloured house (*second from right*). No. 17 Changegate, to the right of the lamp post, was the home of John Wood. He was a cabinet maker and a grandson of William Wood.

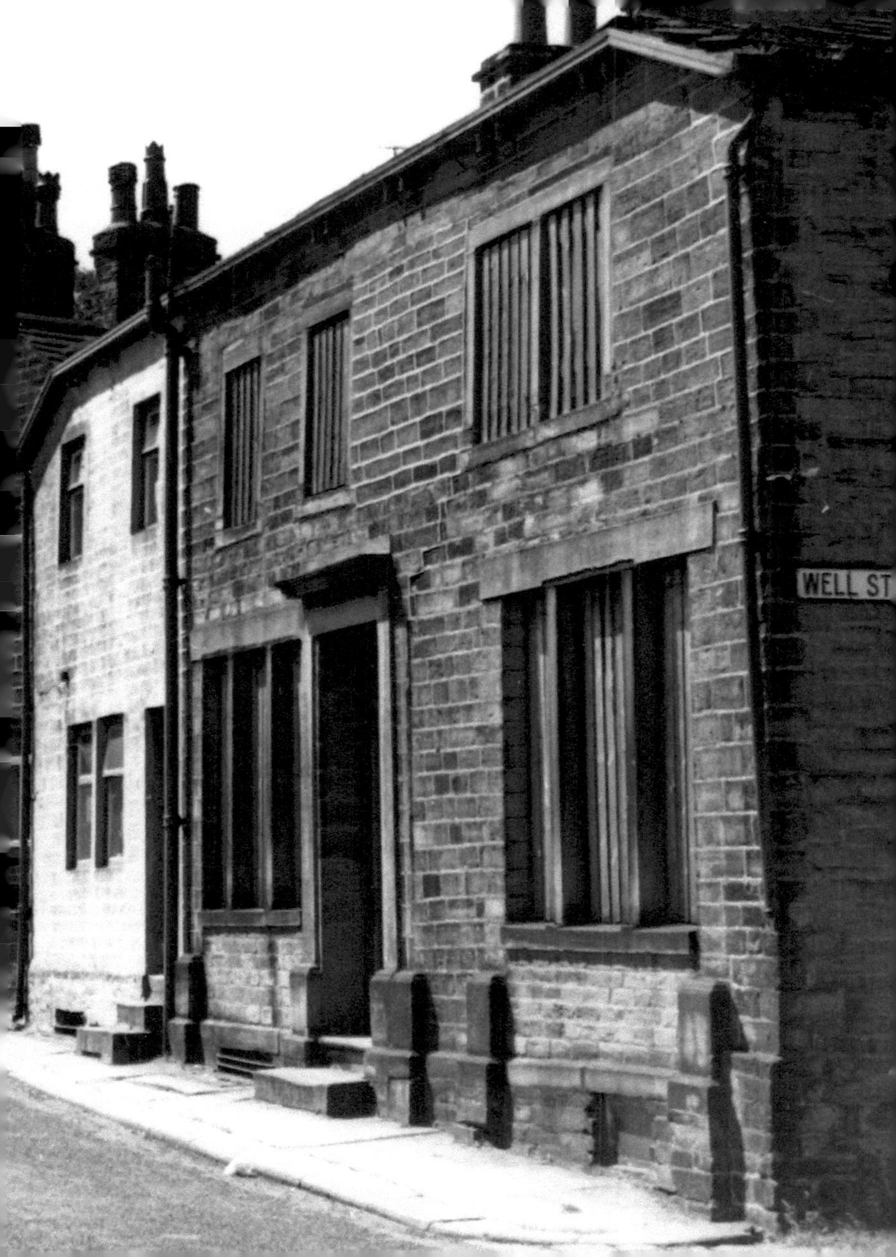
WELL ST

# 39. WELL STREET

Well Street was another casualty of clearance mania. The name comes from three large stone water troughs that used to be there. This Head Well was the main source of water for the upper part of the village in the first half of the nineteenth century. It was inadequate – people had to queue up from two in the morning to get water – and was sometimes so foul that cattle refused to drink from it.

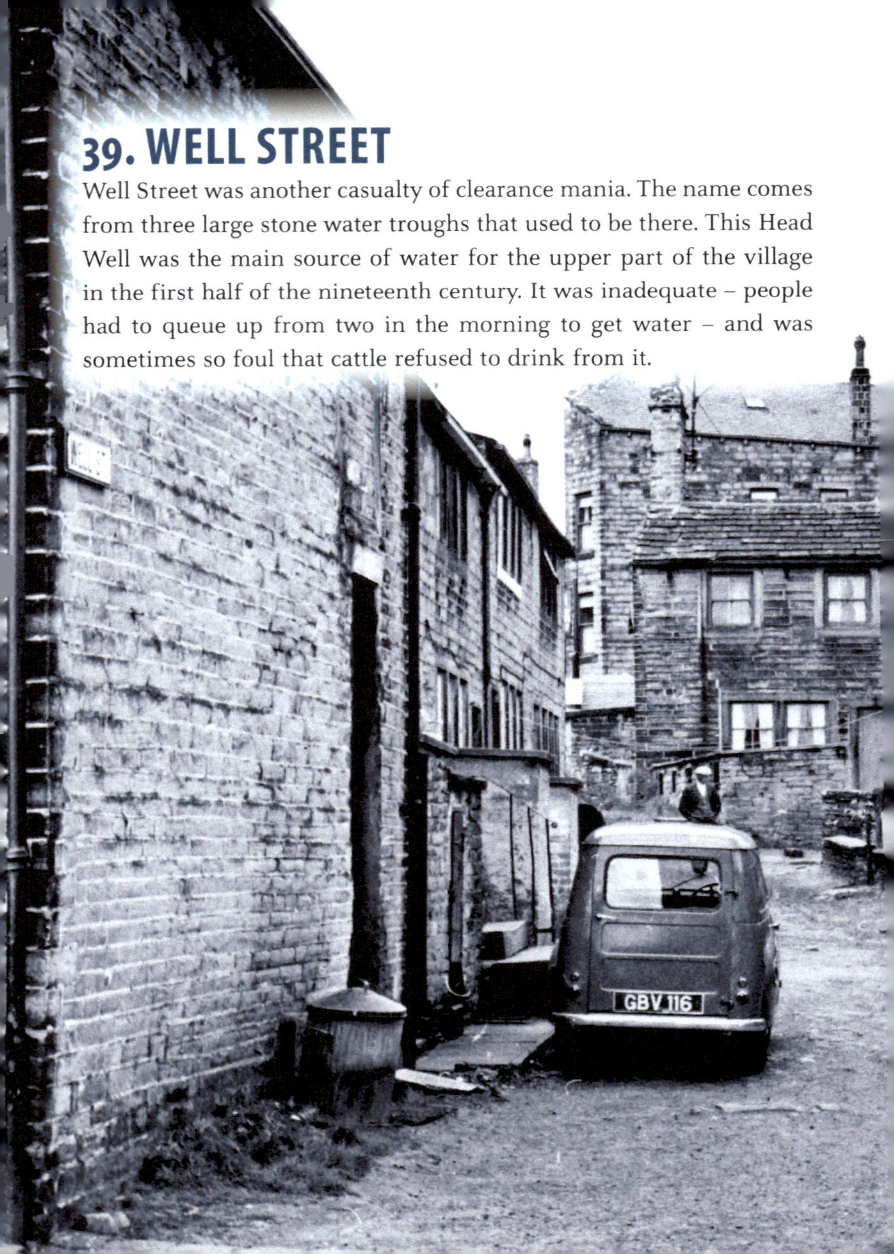

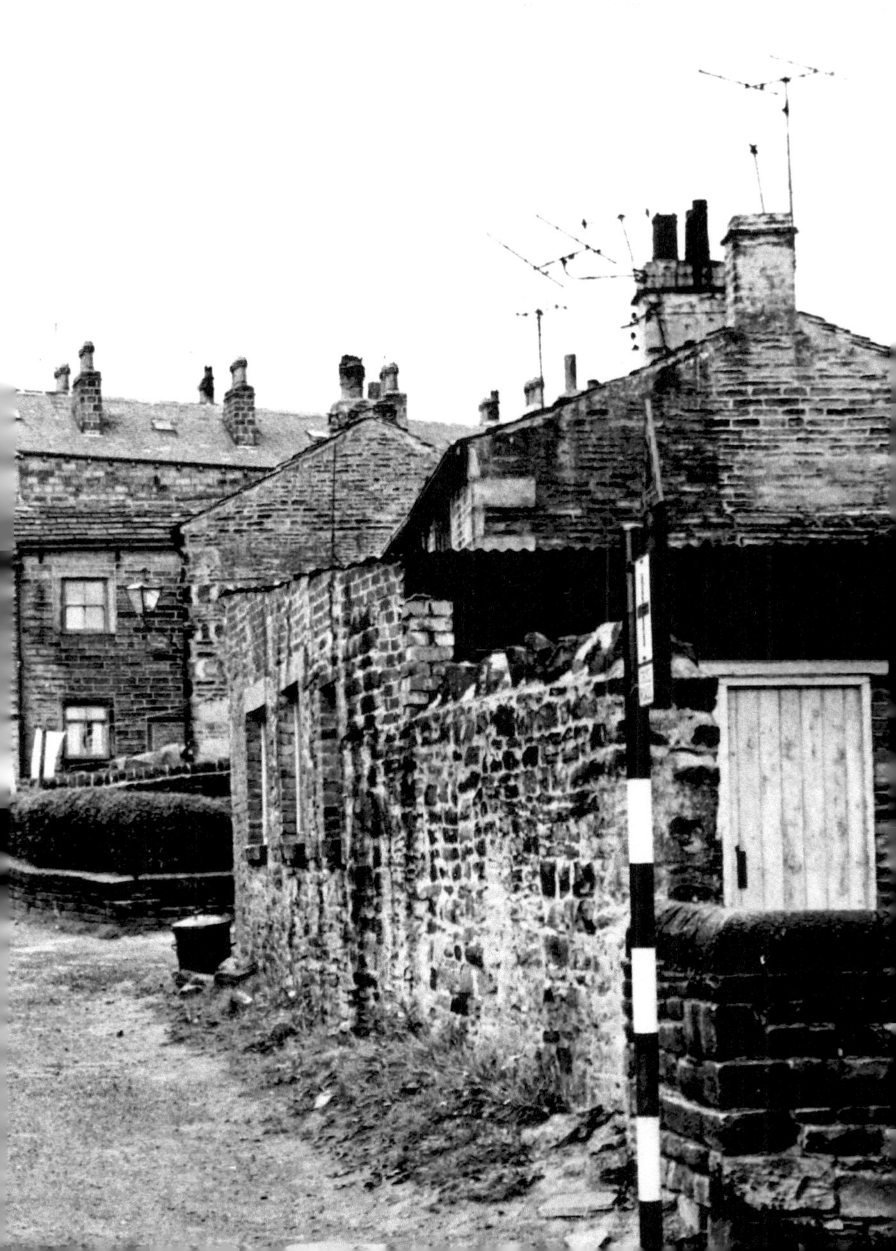

# 40. SPRING HEAD MILL

In the Worth Valley between Haworth and Oakworth is Springhead Mill. The mill was one of three in the area run by the firm of Hattersley, Sons & Co. On the right is a three-storey spinning mill with weaving sheds to the left. The mill chimney rises at the end of the boiler house and engine house. A second spinning mill is behind the chimney and the mill owner's house behind that.

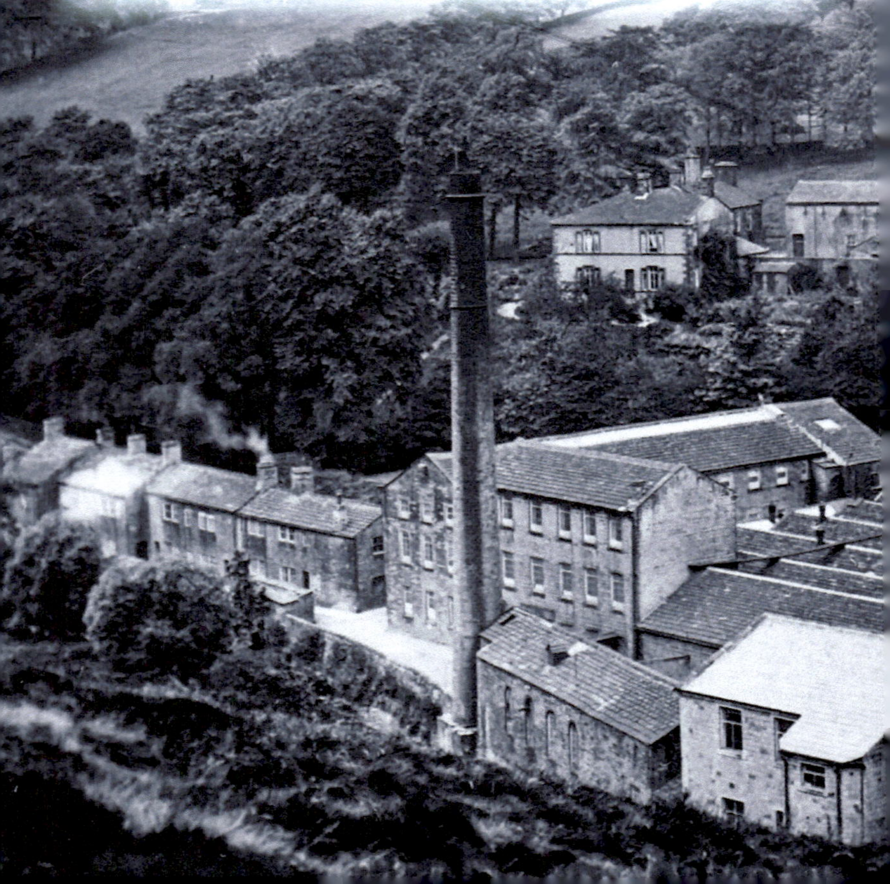

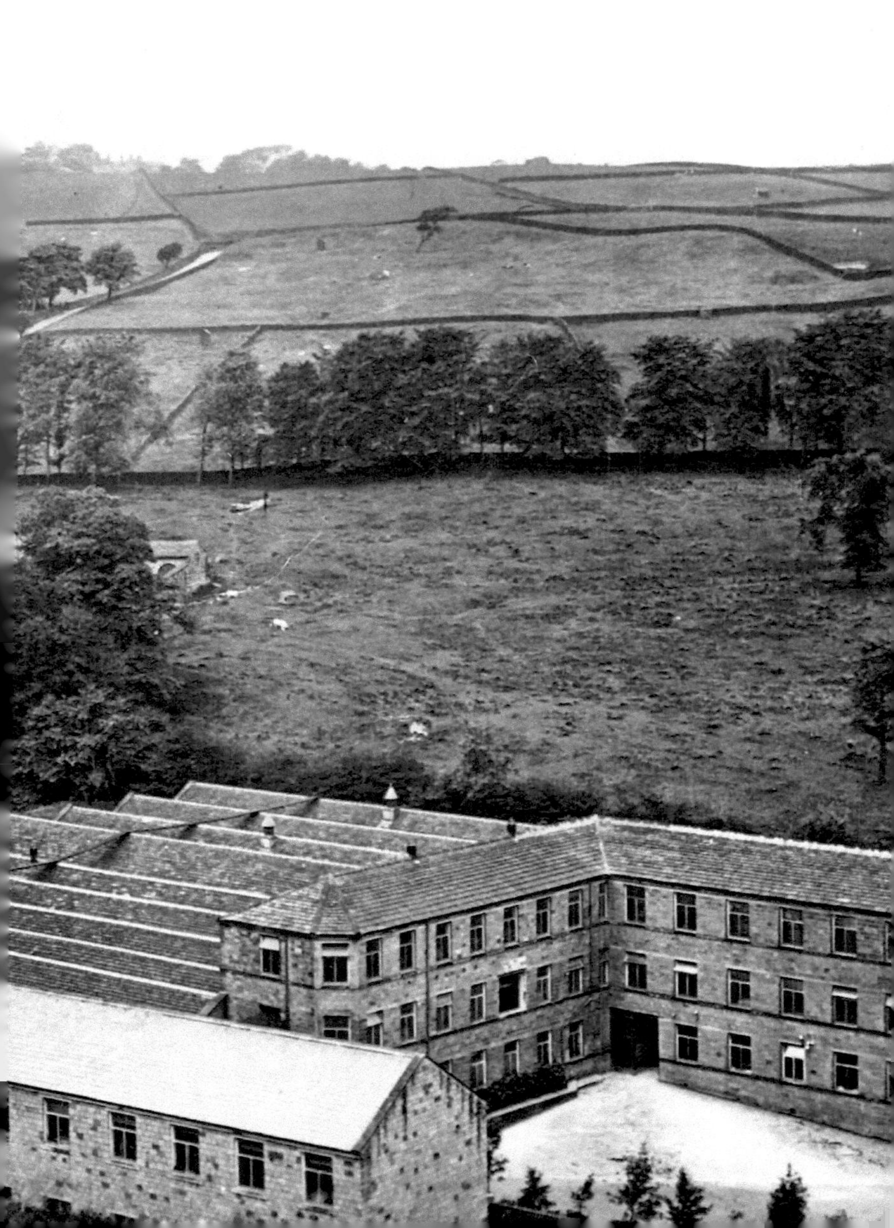

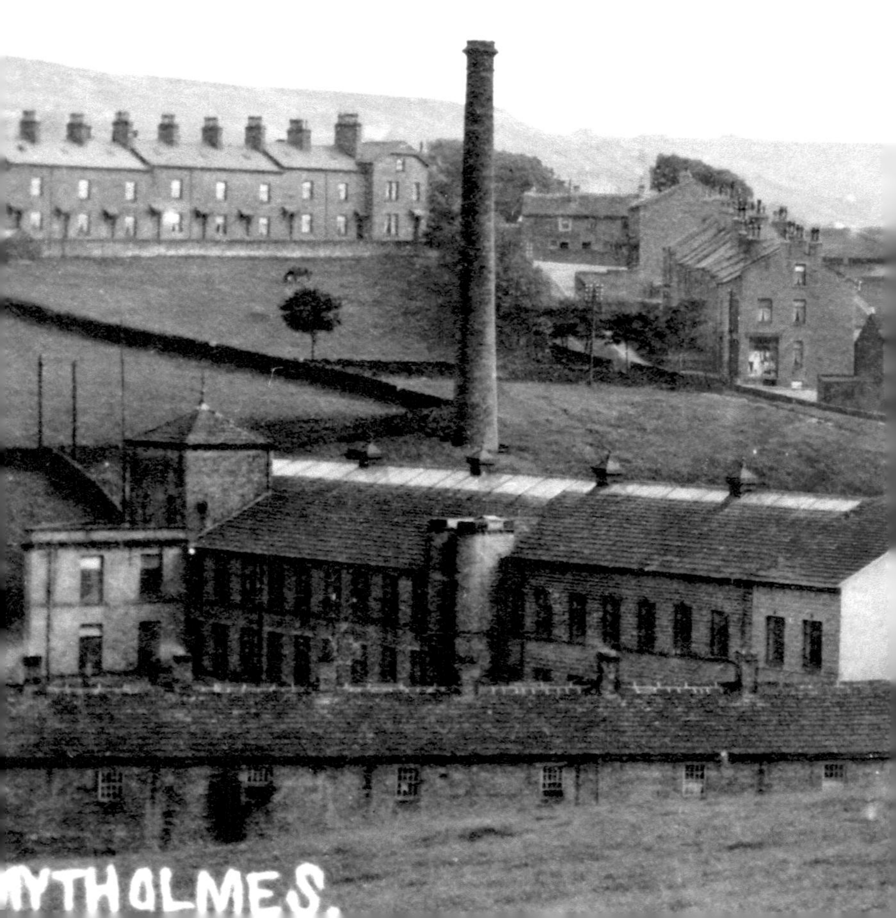
MYTHOLMES.

# 41. MYTHOLMES MILL

Mytholmes was another of the Hattersley mills in the Worth Valley. The trough and chimney show that both steam and water power were used; the waterwheel was removed in 1908. Most of the housing in this picture was built by the firm for their workers between 1835 and 1899. There was also a co-op, other shops, canteen, bath house, tennis courts, bowling green and a mission chapel. Mytholmes was effectively a self-contained mill village.

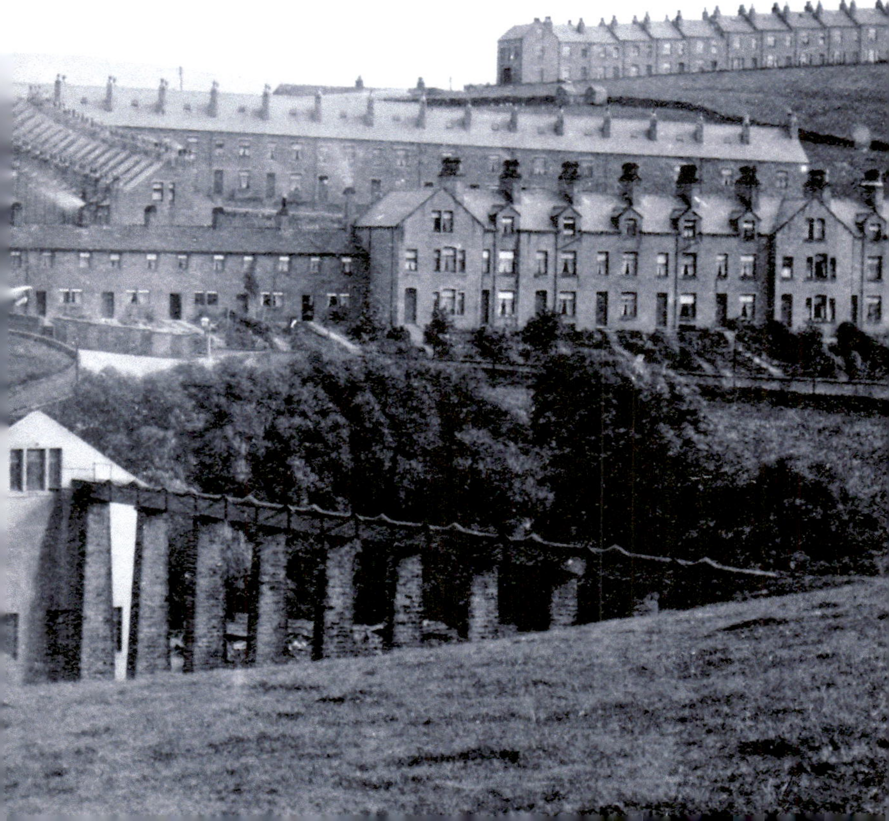

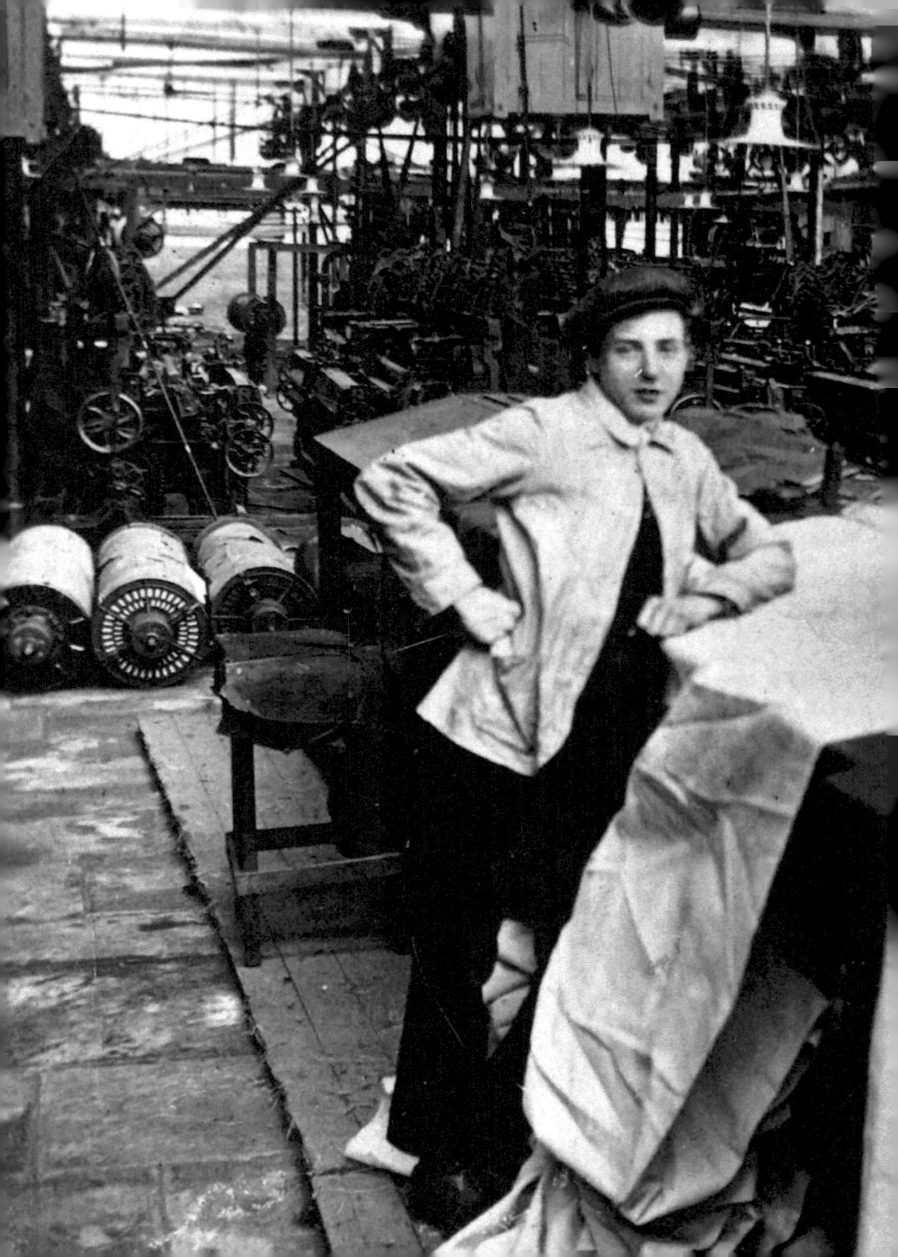

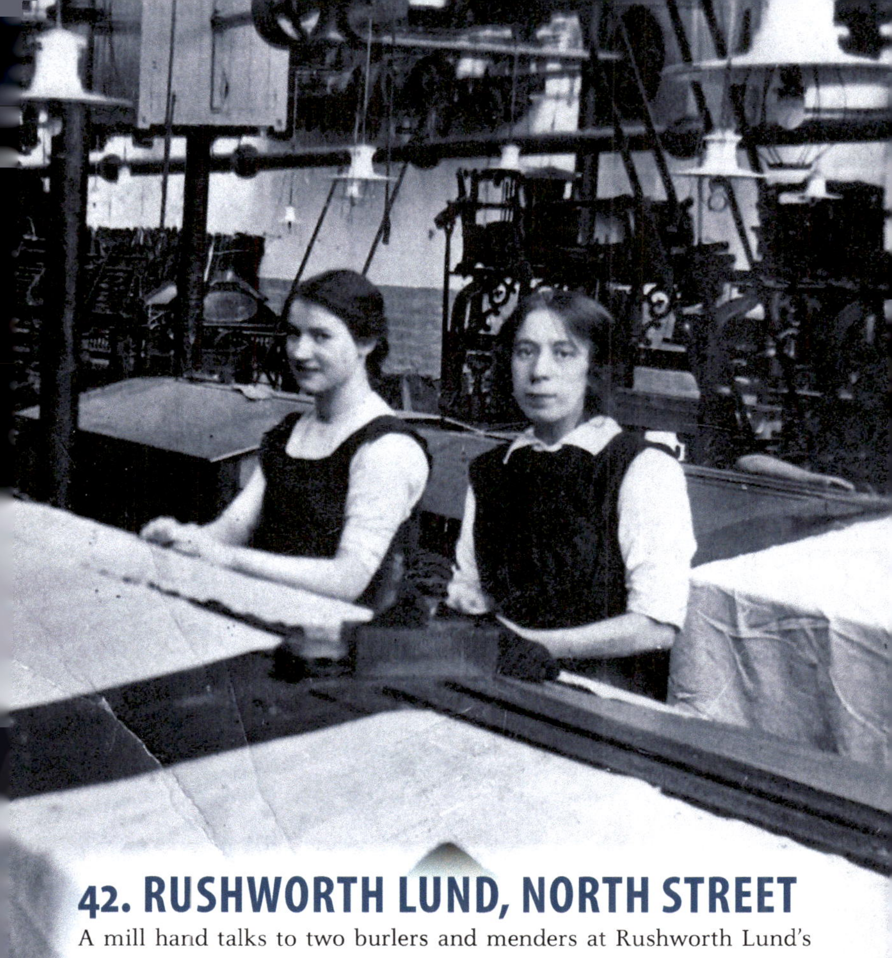

# 42. RUSHWORTH LUND, NORTH STREET

A mill hand talks to two burlers and menders at Rushworth Lund's small worsted mill. Behind them are the looms on which this cloth was woven. Overhead is the line shafting bringing power to the looms. The power source was probably a gas engine as there was no mill chimney and therefore no boiler house for steam generation. A mill shop now occupies these sheds and Townend Farm barn, behind which they lie.

# 43. TOWNEND FARM

Townend Farm is one of Haworth's few seventeenth-century buildings. Dating from around 1600, it is built to an uncommon plan mostly found in the Burnley area. It was among the properties that were bought by the Emmott family in 1749. The barn on the right is that which formed part of Rushworth Lund's mill.

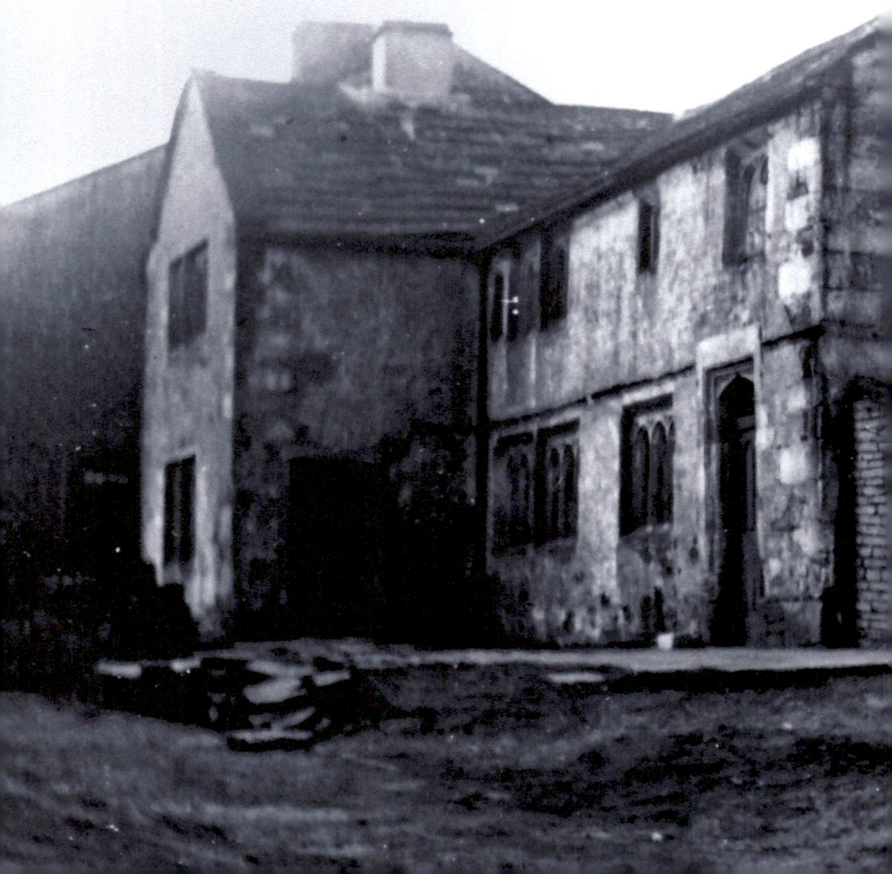

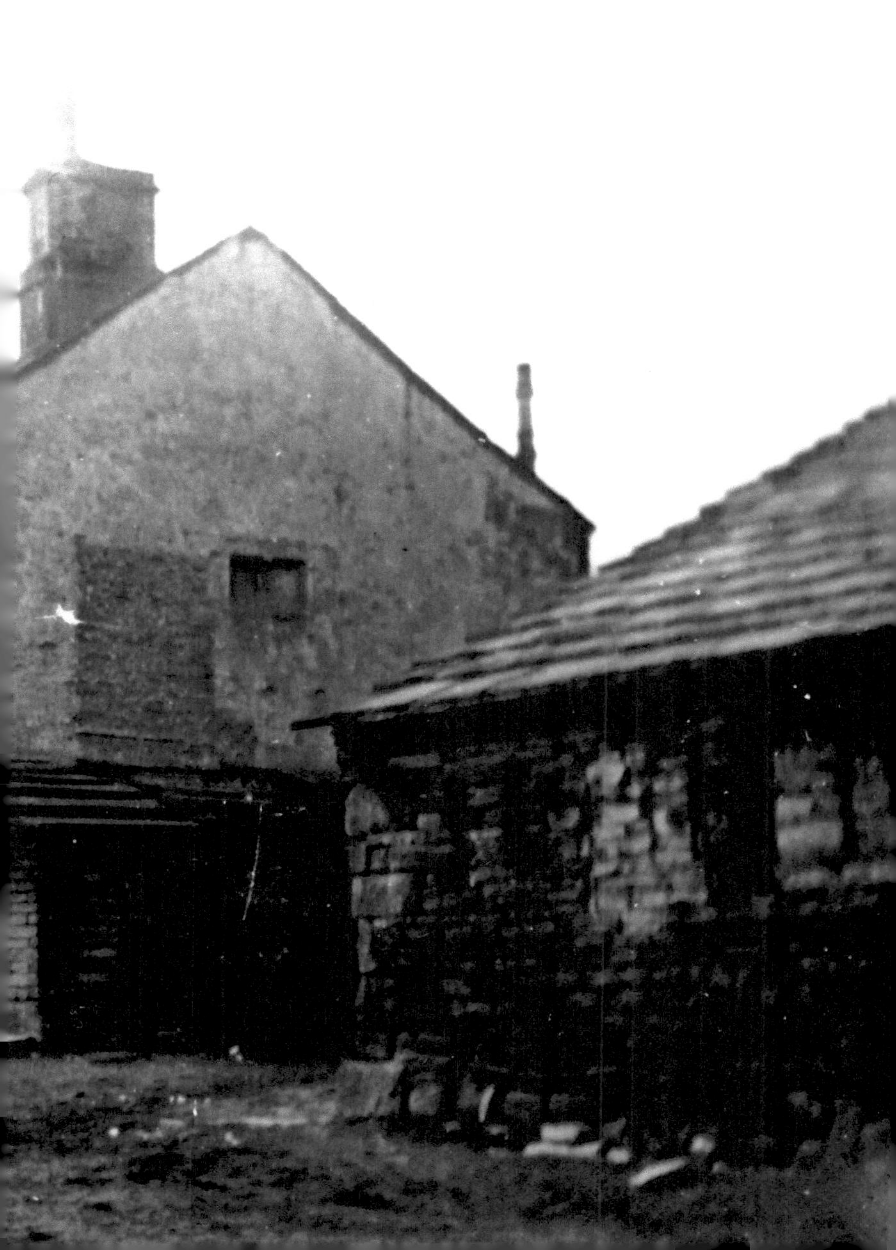

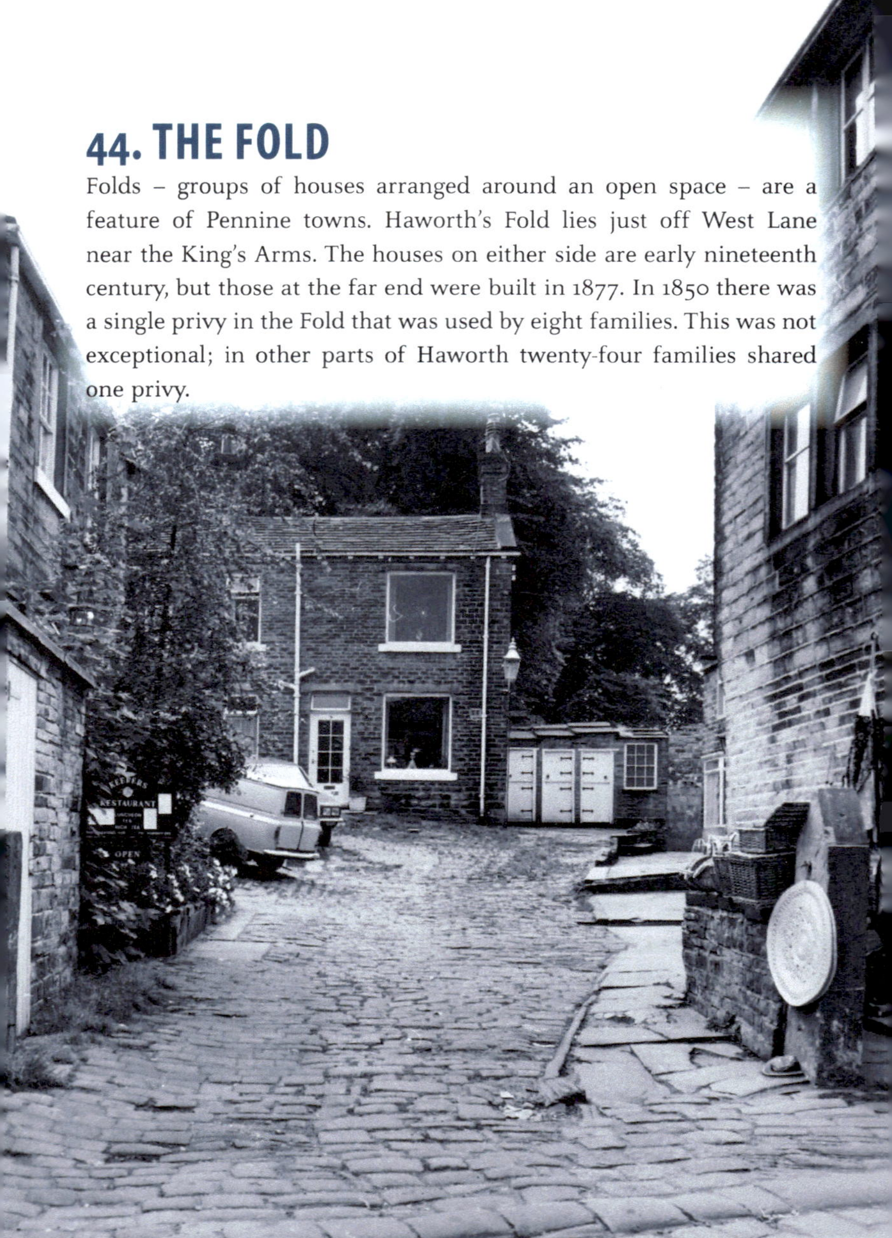


# 44. THE FOLD

Folds – groups of houses arranged around an open space – are a feature of Pennine towns. Haworth's Fold lies just off West Lane near the King's Arms. The houses on either side are early nineteenth century, but those at the far end were built in 1877. In 1850 there was a single privy in the Fold that was used by eight families. This was not exceptional; in other parts of Haworth twenty-four families shared one privy.

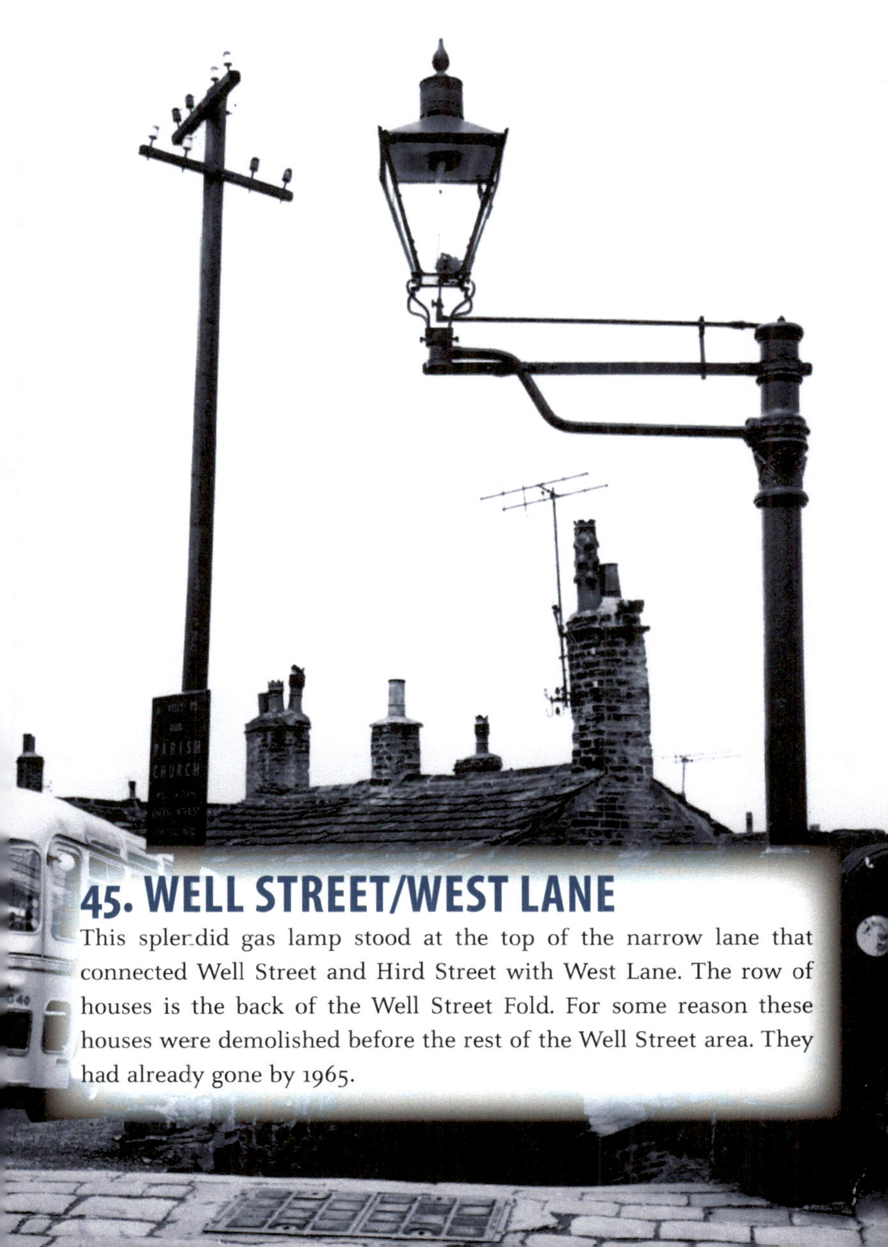

# 45. WELL STREET/WEST LANE

This splendid gas lamp stood at the top of the narrow lane that connected Well Street and Hird Street with West Lane. The row of houses is the back of the Well Street Fold. For some reason these houses were demolished before the rest of the Well Street area. They had already gone by 1965.

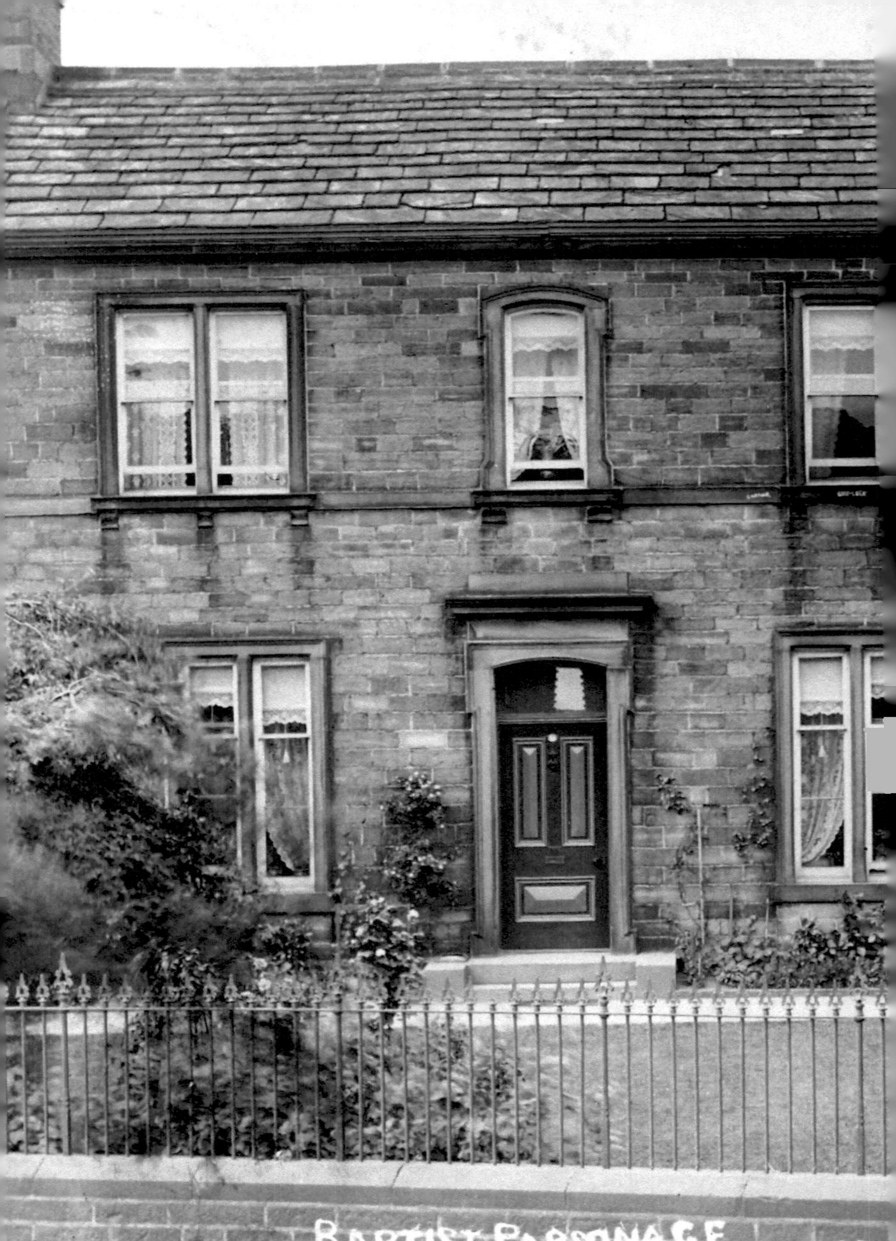
BAPTIST PARSONAGE

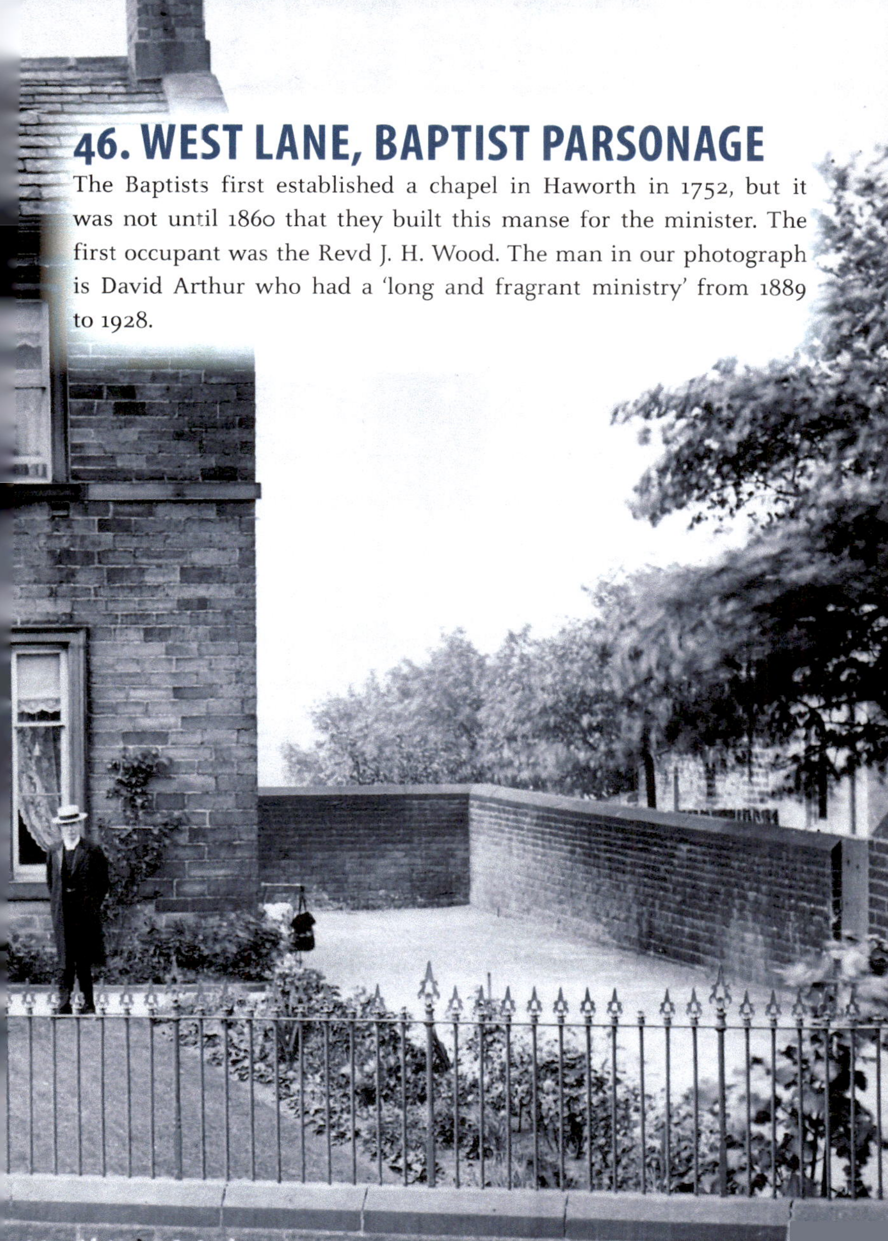

# 46. WEST LANE, BAPTIST PARSONAGE

The Baptists first established a chapel in Haworth in 1752, but it was not until 1860 that they built this manse for the minister. The first occupant was the Revd J. H. Wood. The man in our photograph is David Arthur who had a 'long and fragrant ministry' from 1889 to 1928.

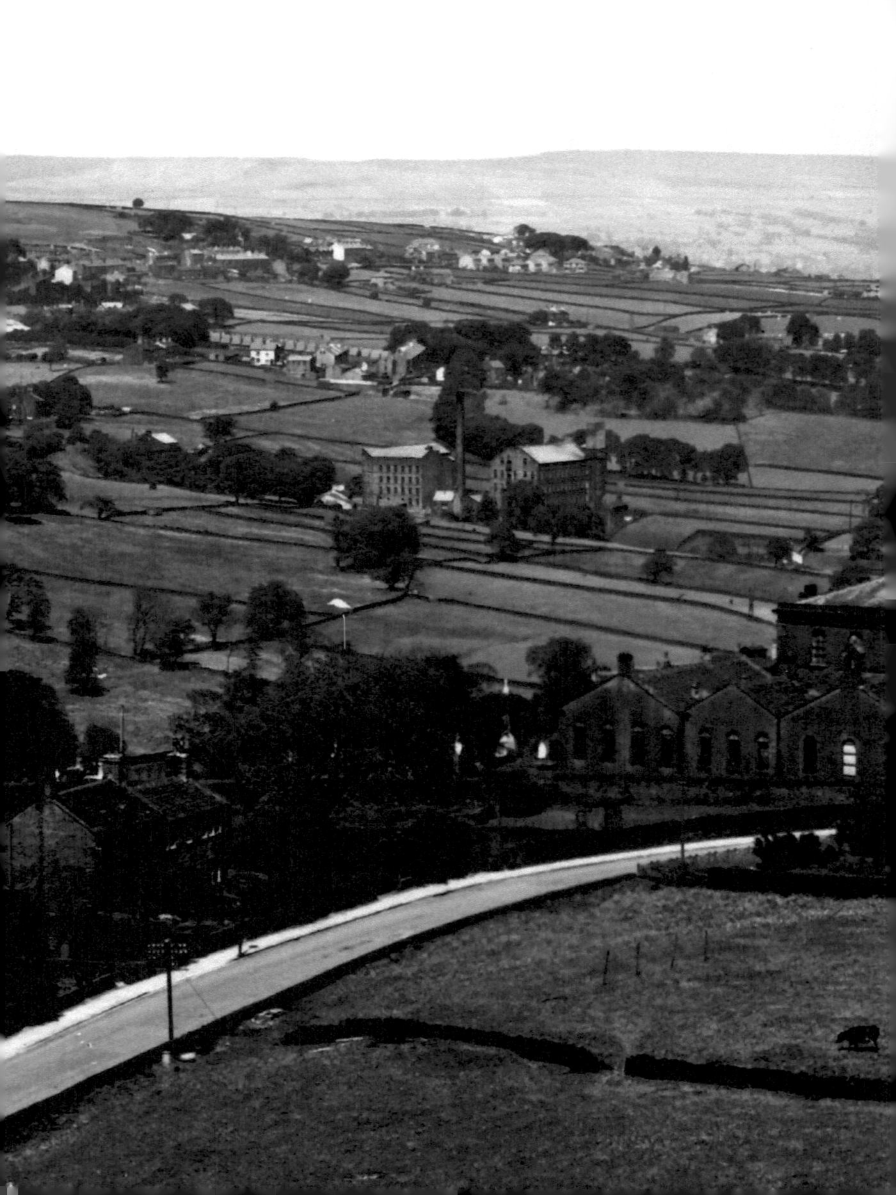

# 47. WEST LANE

A view along West Lane towards the village taken from the edge of Penistone Hill. The narrow field strips in the right foreground are probably part of the medieval arable land of Haworth. The large detached house in the strip with trees and shrubs is the new rectory, which housed Haworth's rectors from 1928, when the old parsonage opened as the Brontë Society's museum, until 2008.

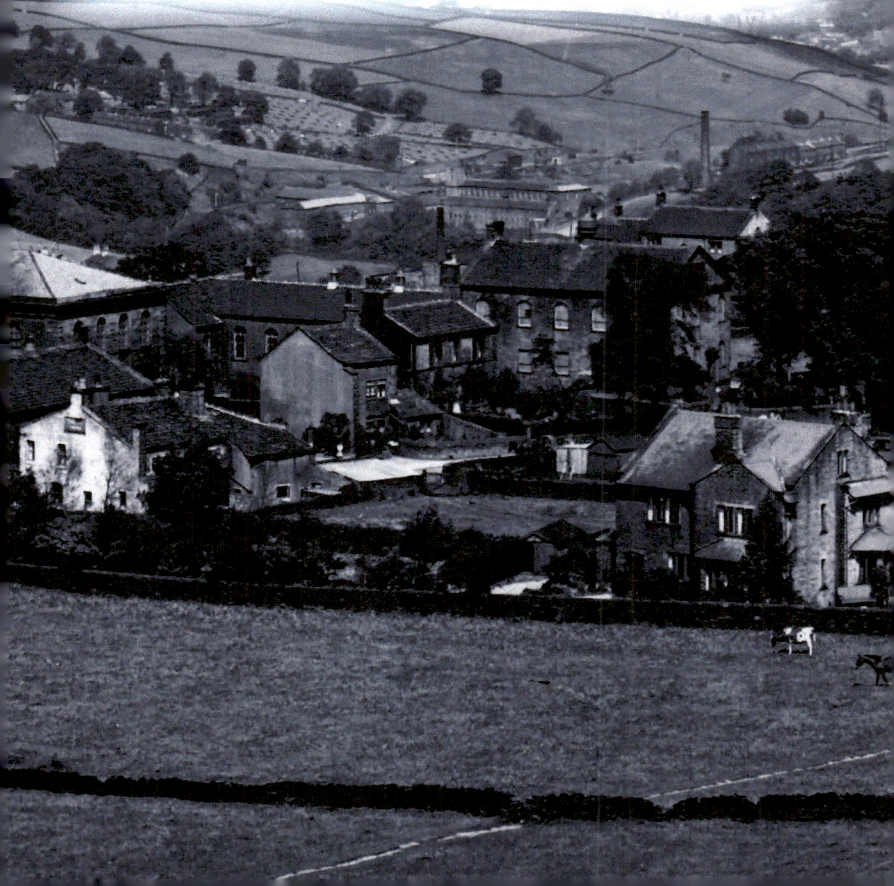

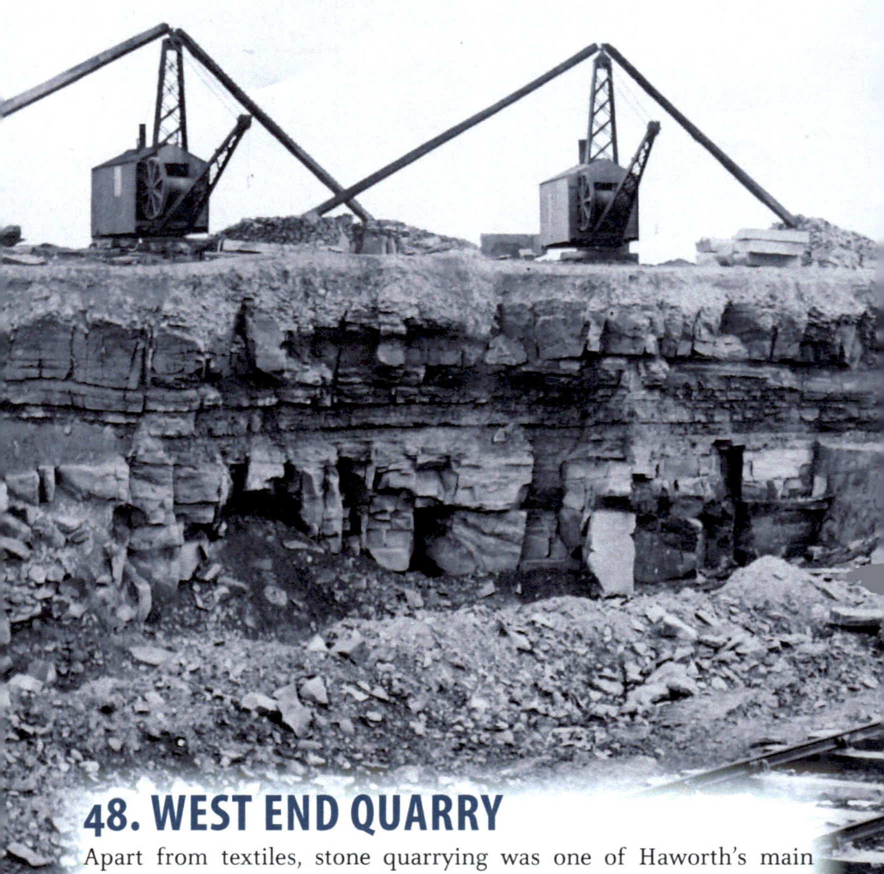

# 48. WEST END QUARRY

Apart from textiles, stone quarrying was one of Haworth's main industries. There are good building stones, flagstones and even roofing stone to be found in the millstone grit. West End quarry was one of four major quarries on Penistone Hill. Large blocks of stone were lifted out of the quarry by the fixed and travelling cranes seen here. The quarry, like nearly all those in the area, is now partially filled in and largely overgrown.

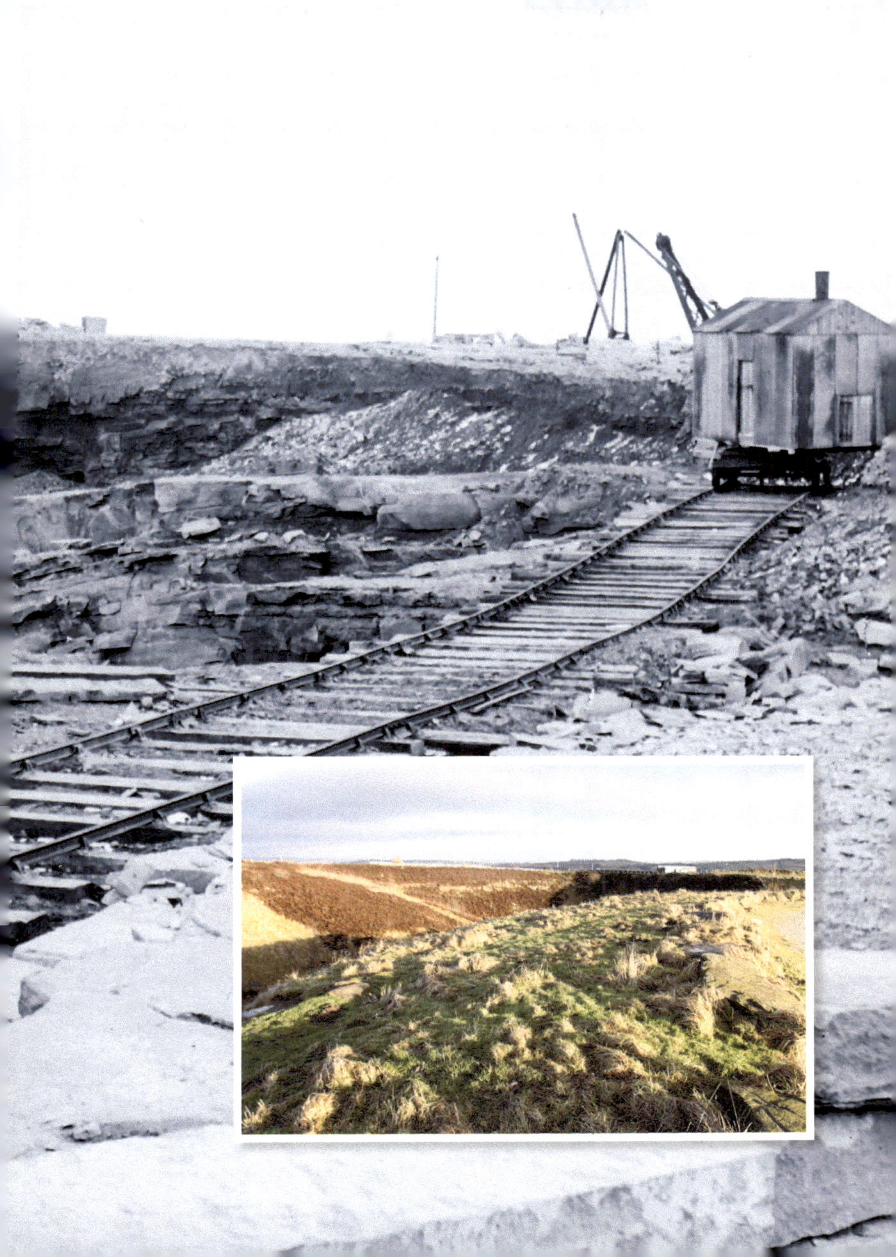

# ACKNOWLEDGEMENTS

I would like to thank the following who have helped with finding old photographs and by providing information about them: The late Eric Bates, Michael Baumber, Bradford Central Library, Robert Buckley, The Civic Trust, Malcolm Craven, Shirley Davids, Molly Davidson, Ann Dinsdale, Anne Dransfield, the late Edward Fearnside, Robin Greenwood, Mary Hatchard, Janet Holdsworth, the late Harold Horsman, Steve Hume, Keighley Local Studies Library, Eddie Kelly, John and Barbara Laycock, the late Jack Laycock, the late Ronnie Mace, Wendy Myers, Bill and the late Ada Parker, the late Mary Preston, David Smith, Michael Smith, Peter Snaith, the late Michael Snowden, Eric Stoney, the late Flossie Waddington, Stephen Whitehead and all the others who have helped over the years.